HOW TO

→ THE COMPLETE GUIDE TO

HAVE A

→ MAKING YOUR IDEAS HAPPEN

HAPPY

→ BEC EVANS

HUSTLE

ICON

This edition published in the UK and USA in 2020 by
Icon Books Ltd, Omnibus Business Centre,
39–41 North Road, London N7 9DP
email: info@iconbooks.com
www.iconbooks.com

Sold in the UK, Europe and Asia by
Faber & Faber Ltd, Bloomsbury House,
74–77 Great Russell Street,
London WC1B 3DA or their agents

Distributed in the UK, Europe and Asia by
Grantham Book Services
Trent Road, Grantham NG31 7XQ

Distributed in the USA
by Publishers Group West,
1700 Fourth Street, Berkeley, CA 94710

Distributed in Canada by Publishers Group Canada,
76 Stafford Street, Unit 300
Toronto, Ontario M6J 2S1

Distributed in Australia and New Zealand by
Allen & Unwin Pty Ltd,
PO Box 8500, 83 Alexander Street,
Crows Nest, NSW 2065

Distributed in India by
Penguin Books India,
7th Floor, Infinity Tower – C, DLF Cyber City,
Gurgaon 122002, Haryana

Distributed in South Africa by
Jonathan Ball, Office B4, The District,
41 Sir Lowry Road, Woodstock 7925

ISBN: 978-178578-593-1

Printed and bound in Great Britain
by Clays Ltd, Elcograf S.p.A.

Contents

SECTION 3: MAKING IDEAS HAPPEN

ABOUT THE AUTHOR

Bec Evans is a writer, speaker, innovation coach and startup founder. While working as a senior manager in publishing she turned her side hustle Prolifiko into a startup. As a consultant she helps businesses innovate and coaches people to build the skills and confidence to make their ideas happen. You can find her on Twitter @Eva_Bec.

Author photo © Sarah Mason Photography

FOREWORD BY VIKAS SHAH MBE
CEO, SWISCOT GROUP

'Hustle' is a strange word. It used to be most commonly associated with aggression, illicit activity (*to hustle money from someone*), or with levels of great activity (*the hustle and bustle of a city*). As with so many words, however, popular culture has chewed it up, and spat it out as something else.

I started my first business when I was still, basically, a kid. I was fourteen and had started building websites in my spare time for local businesses. I just picked up a phone book and tried everything I could to get a deal, and eventually that business grew into an international company which spun out a number of other businesses. This all happened while I was going through my teens and early twenties. For me, *hustle* was simply the act of getting shit done – it was the process of having an idea, taking it to market and learning how to make it happen (usually on the fly)!

It's strange that in recent times the word 'hustle' has turned into something toxic. Social media is full of so-called influencers who tell people to get up at some ungodly hour, never rest, always work and party hard. The problem is that this is not hustle – it's *stupidity*. It's a caricature of a warped fantasy of business – depicting a life that would burn out even the most resilient person.

Don't get me wrong, business is hard. Running your own business or having a side gig is time-consuming, at times soul-destroying, and stressful. However, running your own business can be one of the most profoundly satisfying and stimulating careers, even if – as is the reality – the overwhelming majority of business owners don't get rich from their venture, and a large number 'fail'. (Neither of these outcomes is a reason not to start in the first place ...)

So much commentary on entrepreneurship and business today is based on the *outcome* – how they 'made it' – rather than the *process*. This overlooks a very important aspect: the possibility of having a *happy* hustle.

Bec Evans has built a career out of helping people make their ideas happen. In this book she takes us on a journey from having ideas to polishing them up to making them a reality. This may seem unremarkable in a business book, but what *is* remarkable is that Bec focusses on how to build your idea, have a side gig or develop a startup *without harming yourself in the process*. This book is filled with real-world examples and commentary from founders and experts, and is built on a sturdy skeleton of philosophies and positive psychology – it urges us to remember that fulfilment comes from striving, not from the end result.

Over the past decade, I have been lucky enough to mentor hundreds of startup and scale-up entrepreneurs, many of whom have succeeded, and many of whom haven't – such is the roll of the dice in business. Disappointingly, I have also met hundreds more who had seemingly great ideas and passion who never made it over that first hurdle. As Bec herself says: 'Making ideas happen is hard, and when 90 per cent of startups fail, it's far easier to daydream and never take the risk ...'

I hope many more *do* take the risk thanks to reading *How to Have a Happy Hustle*. Ultimately, it's businesses big and small that make our economies work and generate the innovations that improve our societies each and every day.

My advice? Get reading, and get *hustling*.

Introduction

TO BE HAPPY

At school, when asked what I wanted to be when I grew up, I replied that I wanted to be happy.

Not a helpful response for my teacher who was desperately trying to organise my Year 10 work placement. As a result, while my friends were channelling career goals by pulling on disposable gloves at the vets or chasing copy deadlines at the local paper, I spent the week working in a carpet shop. Unable to sell carpets, fit underlay, or do anything remotely useful, I failed to gain any adult life skills that week, though I did have a laugh with the carpet fitters.

Would that make me happy? It's the sort of question that has bothered philosophers for millennia. Take nineteenth-century thinker John Stuart Mill, who wrote that happy people are those:

> 'who have their minds fixed on some object other than their own happiness; on the happiness of others, on the improvement of mankind, even on some art or pursuit, followed not as a means, but as itself an ideal end. Aiming thus at something else, they find happiness by the way.'[1]

What Mill means is that the fulfilling kind of happiness – not the wave-your-arms-in-the-air-like-you-just-don't-care hedonistic kind, but the stuff that will keep you going long term – doesn't happen when you aim for it. Happiness happens when you're doing something else, ideally something with a purpose. While office banter passes the time when you're trapped in a daily drudge, the frequency of workplace giggles isn't the kind of happiness that keeps us engaged in our work. Stop wasting time and instead make some art, build something or help others.

HUSTLING YOUR WAY TO FULFILMENT

Many of us want to do and be more. We want to have ideas, create something new, go beyond the confines of our job and start something of our own.

Researching this book, I asked people why they wanted to get their ideas into the world. What surprised me was that most didn't want extra cash, to gain new skills for a promotion or to leave their current job, or even to start a new business. Instead, the top reason given – by a long shot – was self-fulfilment (otherwise known as happiness).

What would I tell my teenage self, kicking her heels in a carpet shop? I'd tell her this: while being happy is a laudable aim, it will escape your clutches if you reach for it alone. True fulfilment only comes as a byproduct of doing something which stretches you. I'd tell myself to find a side hustle.

Helping you find your hustle is what this book is all about.

If you have a vague ambition or an inkling of an idea, pursue it, even if it might fail, because you'll find happiness along the way, often in ways you weren't expecting. This book is for you if:

- You dream of having ideas but don't know how to start.

- You have the beginning of concept but got stuck making it happen.

- You imagine fulfilment lies beyond the 9–5 career-track but don't know where to look.

- You have an aspiration for a side hustle or startup but lack the confidence, skills, time or money.

HOW TO HAVE A HAPPY HUSTLE

I'm not going to sugar-coat it. Making ideas happen is tough – that's why it's a *hustle*. Hustling involves time, effort and hard work, often done as a side project alongside your other commitments.

Even if you have a corker of a concept, it's tough developing it and getting it into the world, and when it's there, it might not find a market. If you're hankering for startup success, you're best placing your bets elsewhere as the odds are stacked against you – the sad fact is 90 per cent of startups will fail.

The point of a happy hustle is not that it's hard (there are enough startup books about that) but that trying to make ideas happen will give you great pleasure and fulfilment.

There are five principles that underpin a happy hustle:

1. **Dream big but start small**. Ambition is great – it gets us out of bed in the morning and striving for more. But without a plan, your dreams can come to nothing. You have to start. And by starting small you bypass the fear centres of the

brain, lower the stakes, and are more likely to rack up the wins that will keep you motivated, positive and moving forward.

2. **Don't fall in love with your idea**. Founder bias can blind you to feedback and keep you forging ahead with a failed plan when the evidence tells you to quit. Instead, fall in love with the problem your idea solves. Fall in love with the people who have the problem and the customers who use your solution – they will guide you to a better idea.

3. **Ship before you're ready**. Forget perfectionism – you don't have the time or money to keep tinkering. Make something and get it out to people quickly and often. Think of each version as an experiment to gather data to inform what you're doing next. By having tight feedback loops you learn fast and improve your idea as it takes shape in the world.

4. **Connect with others**. Working in isolation is the worst thing you can do for your idea's survival. So, find friends and peers who can support you, early users who can test and feed back, communities of people who are interested in what you do, and networks of people on a similar journey. Relationships will help you and your idea thrive.

5. **Focus on the process not the outcome**. Most ideas will fail, so don't aim for a narrow end point of success. As you build and test your idea, learn from the experience, notice what you enjoy, reflect on what works and what you'd like to do more of, seek out engagement, and be motivated by what excites, challenges

and stimulates you. And when things go wrong, you'll have the resilience to keep going.

These approaches will help you overcome the barriers many of us face when starting something. They will help you start, build momentum and keep going. You just need to start.

SO, WHAT'S STOPPING YOU?

You might be thinking: it's all well and good taking small steps and learning along the way, but how the hell am I going to find the time?

You're right, your life is full of important and urgent things to do. 'Busy' doesn't even describe the demands on your time and attention. To fit a side project into your schedule you must make the time. That isn't easy. It involves saying 'no' to nice offers, setting boundaries, and reprioritising what's in your schedule so there's space to make things happen.

Let's dive in with a quick exercise. Think: how do you currently spend your time? Look back on the past week and consider what's getting your attention or, even better, log your day-to-day activity as you do it to build up an accurate picture. Then, imagine you could re-live that week bearing in mind your current commitments. How would you reorganise your schedule? What different choices would you make with your time? Were there opportunities you missed to work on your idea? Hindsight is indeed a wonderful thing.

With that knowledge in mind, let's look ahead. Plan when you can make time. Grab your calendar or draw a weekly schedule like the one below:

- Fill in days across the top and your normal waking hours down the side.

- Block out all the times you are already committed to things like work, childcare, exercise.

- What's left? Are there any opportunities? If yes, book in some idea time.

- Not found any time? Reschedule other tasks to free up time. What can you stop doing or delegate? Can you get up earlier, go to work later? This is tough, but you can do it.

- Commit to your schedule. Book time for your idea like any other appointment and don't get distracted.

⏱	Sun	Mon	Tues
6·00	↑ 𝗓ᶻ		
7·00	sleep	breakfast	breakfast
8·00	↓	commute	commute
9·00	(FAMILY)	WORK	WORK
10·00	TIME		
11·00	boxercise	↓	↓
12·00	↑ lunch	lunch	lunch
13·00	↓	WORK	WORK
14·00	↑ Kids do		
15·00	↓ homework		
16·00	TV +		
17·00	CHILL	↓	↓
18·00	Dinner	commute	commute
19·00	school bag	cook/eat	cook/eat
20·00	TV +	TV	TV
21·00	CHILL	TV	TV

get up early

take longer lunch → go to cafe

while dinner cooks + kids watch TV 📺

Don't watch TV !!

The internet is full of self-proclaimed productivity gurus sharing their secret to making time; often it involves getting up at the godforsaken hour of 5am.

Great for them, but it might not work for you, your family and your well-being.

No one knows how long it will take you to make your idea happen – just as your idea is unique, so is your approach to creating it. The goal is to make progress regularly, so don't worry about project planning just yet, and instead build momentum bit by bit.

I've found four distinct time patterns to how people move their passion projects and side hustles ahead.

1. The **daily doer** has a regular routine, often working in the same time and place, to nudge forward their idea.

2. The **scheduler** looks ahead a week or two and blocks time into their calendar. They take a realistic and practical approach to planning and getting things done.

3. The **spontaneous hustler** grabs any opportunity as it appears, making the most of delayed trains, cancelled meetings and sleeping children.

4. The **binger**'s life is chock-full, so instead of a daily or weekly hustle, they binge every month or so on uninterrupted deep work, a progress-making day or days that are as productive as they are rare.

There is no one-size-fits-all approach to making time; the important thing is just to do it. Don't feel bad when you really don't have the time, but make the most of when you do. You'll surprise yourself by what you can achieve, even when you're feeling tired and uninspired. While common sense suggests that you create best when you're at your most alert and awake, researchers have found the opposite, saying that:

'tasks involving creativity might benefit from a non-optimal time of day.'[2] Perhaps those internet gurus were right about 5am after all?

Now you've found some time, read on to get the inside track on what to do and how other people have done it.

This book shares tried and tested techniques from my work in business innovation to turn you into an ideas machine. I'll guide you step by step with super-practical advice to build your skills and confidence as you make things happen. The book uses my experience turning a side hustle into a startup, alongside stories of founders who have led the way, so you can learn from others' success – and failures. It is supported by expert advice and research-backed tips on how to make the most of the process.

I'll show you how to be happy as you work to make your idea happen, regardless of whether your idea fails or takes off.

Let's get to it. It's time to hustle.

1 Having ideas

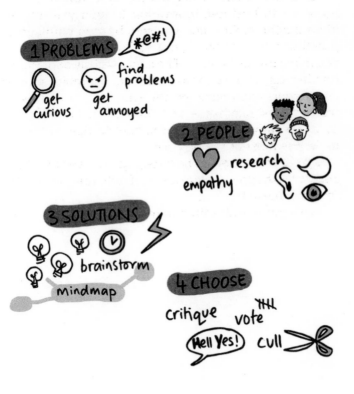

CHAPTER ONE

Problems

It all started, much like every other day, with Jo Caley getting dressed. That fateful morning, she put her foot through the knee of her favourite pair of jeans, ripping them beyond repair. Her jeans were wrecked but she was about to discover her big idea – and it all began with her hatred of shopping.

'I was gutted,' she says. 'I'd have to spend hours traipsing around the shops feeling inadequate, that nothing fits me, and I can't afford anything that I like.'

To avoid the misery of the high street, Caley decided to buy her jeans online, but the more websites she searched the more confusing it got.

To understand why she hates shopping, take a peek inside her wardrobe. Open the doors and you'll find clothes ranging in size from a UK 6 to 14. Perhaps she's got an issue with her weight, perhaps she's a yo-yo dieter? No, her weight and figure have been consistent for years. Caley's real problem is that in one shop she's petite but when she goes to another shop she's pushing large. Each retailer uses a different set of measurements to clothe her same-sized body. And it's not just interpretation of sizing standards, there are a whole bunch of alternative systems including UK, US and European sizes; small, medium and large options; waist measurement and leg lengths; and then there are shops with their own unique numbering systems.

But, in the midst of her jeans shopping nightmare, her despair turned into curiosity. 'I realised my problem, and then I thought, this is quite interesting. This must be really annoying for everybody, not just me.'

Caley was right. She realised she was part of a much wider trend. Nearly 60 per cent of British women struggle to find the right size clothes.[3] Caley had encountered 'vanity sizing', a problem that millions of women face.

'Poor bloody women,' she tells me. 'Who has time to find a pair of jeans that not only fits them, but fits their budget, that they like the look of, and does everything else that they want a pair of jeans to do?'

She was determined to help. But before we hear about her solution, let's spend a bit more time with her as she stands half dressed, holding her torn jeans, feeling annoyed and upset.

WHY PROBLEMS?

Caley was in the right place to have an idea.

Before you fling off your clothes and wait for inspiration in your underpants, let's find out what that means.

Y Combinator is the largest and most successful startup accelerator in the world. It has helped thousands of people turn their ideas into fast-growing technology businesses worth millions, and its investment portfolio includes big names like

Airbnb, Reddit, Dropbox and Stripe. Its co-founder Paul Graham has simple advice for generating ideas:

> 'The way to get startup ideas is not to try to think of startup ideas. It's to look for problems, preferably problems you have yourself.'[4]

Caley had a problem. She found out other people shared it, and she got super interested in solving it. She did all of that before spending any time generating ideas or finding solutions.

The best way to have an idea is to start with a problem. The best way to find problems is to get curious.

Throughout this book, you will meet people with inspiring side hustles, founders who turned dilemmas into successful startups, professionals who problem-solve for clients every day, and idea-makers who help people to design and create solutions. Together, we'll crush the myth of the lone inventor – because no one plucks fully formed ideas from some mysterious place in the sky. Instead, you'll get a team of advisers with expertise and advice to turn you into an ideas machine.

BE CURIOUS

Have a problem? Don't fret. Be curious instead.

Curiosity will help you hunt down problems and keep you interested as you explore them and decide which one to focus on. Once you've found a problem, you'll generate solutions that people want, need and will pay for.

So, let's get problematic. Over the coming chapter, you'll:

- Stop waiting for inspiration.

- Become a problem seeker and find what's bugging you.

- Choose the most exciting problem.

- Finish up with a problem statement.

DON'T WAIT FOR APPLES TO FALL

Archimedes had a burst of inspiration – a world-changing, knowledge-creating, scientific breakthrough, an idea so fantastic and urgent he leapt out of the bath and ran naked down the street, shouting 'Eureka!' – the ancient Greek for 'I have found it!' Archimedes hadn't found inspiration in the bath tub, but a solution to a problem he'd been desperate to solve.

History is packed full of neat inspiration stories like Archimedes' Eureka moment – take Sir Isaac Newton and his apple-inspired gravity discovery. Beware these myths of invention.

> 'Don't wait for the proverbial apple to fall on your head. Go out in the world and proactively seek experiences that will spark creative thinking. Interact with experts, immerse yourself in unfamiliar environments, and role play customer scenarios. Inspiration is fuelled by a deliberate planned course of action.' [5]

So say David and Tom Kelley, two brothers on a mission to democratise creativity. They trash the myth of a lone creative genius and instead build people's confidence to seek inspiration through an active approach. They have made the process of invention their lives' work, championing human-centred design. David founded D-School at Stanford which, alongside his other founding organisation, the design agency IDEO where his brother Tom also works, has trained a generation of designers around the world to solve problems big and small. Anyone, they believe, can be a creative problem-solver, you just need to start.

Most people talk themselves out of having ideas. They dissuade themselves from starting side hustles. They stop themselves from building businesses. They tell themselves they aren't that sort of person, they don't have the right skills or experience.

You are the right person. You have the right skills. What you're interested in is important, and that puts you in the perfect position to make things happen. I'm going to make sure you have the best advice to get started.

I asked Jenn Maer, who works with the Kelley brothers as senior design director at IDEO, how we can begin. 'It's not so much a process as much as it is a way of looking at the world,' Maer says. 'Keeping an open, creative and optimistic mindset is incredibly important if you want to create change. You have to believe that something can be different before you can actually make it different.'

The creative mindset is a curious one, that wants to see, try, do and learn something new. We all know the advice about taking time away from our screens to take a walk, talk to people, go to an art gallery, or read a magazine or book. So far, so vanilla. I asked Maer what she recommends.

'Look at some weird shit,' she says. This means explore things that challenge you, stimulate your thinking and make you happy. Don't have an agenda – because having an agenda is what kills you.

Agendas are everywhere, in our daily routines and habits. Here's a simple exercise to squash agendas and trigger new experiences: change your morning routine.[6] You could, for example, shake up your work commute by changing transport and cycling instead of getting the train, getting off the bus a stop earlier and walking, driving a different route, or listening to a different podcast or playlist. A small change to your routine can make you see things differently; it will put you in a position of curiosity because you won't be able to rely on your habitual way of engaging with the world.

Getting out of your comfort zone can lead to new discoveries. The research backs this up. Angela Duckworth, professor of psychology at the University of Pennsylvania, writes that:

> 'interests are *not* discovered through introspection. Instead, interests are triggered by interactions with the outside world. The process of interest discovery can be messy, serendipitous, and inefficient. This is because you can't really predict with certainty what will capture your attention and what won't.'[7]

Take Jo Caley. Her interaction with her jeans was certainly messy and inefficient – she stumbled serendipitously in her jeans and ripped her way to an interest. Vanity sizing wasn't something she knew about, or cared about; if you had asked her about it before her jeans incident she might have said she didn't want or need to solve the problem, but once she had experienced the problem, started digging into it, she was hooked.

You can't predict how or when you will find a problem that interests you, but you can open yourself up to spot them. Here's how to be a problem seeker.

WHAT'S YOUR PROBLEM?

Life is full of annoyances.

You get up, burn your toast at breakfast, and wait to board a late-running, overcrowded commuter train whose route is beset by Wi-Fi blackspots; the lack of signal drives you to read the free daily paper over the shoulder of a seated passenger, in which you discover reports of climate collapse, dwindling natural resources and the extinction of species.

Our world is full of flaws. Embrace that imperfection – it will be fuel for your ideas. Tap into your frustration to find problems you care about and want to solve.

Start with what's bugging you now. Problems hit us like a meteor, or we stumble over them regularly – like that step up to the corner shop that you can't get the pushchair over – or they seep into us like a continuous rain.

What problems have you faced today? What got your blood boiling this week? Last week? Last month? Or are you still fuming over a frustration from last year, from college, or childhood? If you've been harbouring it that long it certainly needs fixing.

Collect the problems you experience. Make a note of them. Observe and jot down what you see, without judging. It doesn't matter how big or small the problems are, whether they affect one person or 1 million – just find and record them.

Make a list of ten, 50 or even 100 problems. Start now:

- Go into the world and see what trips you up in your day.

- Stay at home and see what's lurking within your kitchen, bedroom or bathroom.

- Read, watch TV and videos, scroll through social media, play games – however you interact with the real or virtual world.

- Think back over the last few days to find more things that didn't work as they should, the frustrations and annoyances and the plain unexpected broken.

- Delve into the past to dredge up previous issues.

- Ask your friends, family or co-workers what's got them riled. Listen to them – they'll love having your attention. An extra bonus, all this listening will make you more sympathetic as you realise what other people struggle with. More on this in the next chapter.

Gather problems in a notebook or use the notes app on your phone, leave yourself voice memos, or take photos and create an album – whichever way you prefer, record them in some way. Don't let them vanish into thin air.

Get in the habit of gathering problems, noticing stuff that's interesting, weird and doesn't work as it should.

Make it a daily routine. Challenge yourself to record ten problems a day for a week and soon you'll have a notebook bulging with problems waiting to be solved.

And remember, no coming up with solutions yet. The time for ideas will come.

SEEK PROBLEMS, FIND HAPPINESS

Looking for things that make your blood boil might not seem like the route to nirvana, but trust me, finding problems will make you happy. That's because it engages our 'seeking' system which is fuelled by the pleasure-inducing neurotransmitter dopamine.

Seeking is described as the 'granddaddy' of our brain systems by Washington State University neuroscientist Dr Jaak Panksepp, who spent his life researching the neurobiological basis of emotions.

The seeking system is a motivational engine that drives all animals to be interested in the world around them, to go out and explore, and get excited by what they find. Panksepp said: 'it helps fill the mind with interest and motivates organisms to move their bodies effortlessly in search of the things they need, crave, and desire. In humans, this may be one of the main brain systems that generate and sustain curiosity, even for intellectual pursuits.'[8]

For humans, this system takes us beyond animalistic physical survival and into the world of ideas. It motivates us to find problems and keeps us engaged as we try to solve them. Bring on the dopamine.

FOLLOW YOUR CURSES AND FORM A CLUB

When I started working from home, the local couriers designated my house the unofficial delivery office. While my neighbours were off at work and college, I would always be available to accept a delivery.

Every time the doorbell rang, I would leap from my chair, run down two flights of stairs from the office, and race to the always-locked front door.

Now where did I leave my door keys? Let the hunt begin, rummaging through recently used bags and patting down my jacket pockets, checking kitchen surfaces and scanning table tops. Finding my keys was a problem.

Now, my common-sense solution of fitting a hook by the door isn't going to win any innovation awards, but it taught me to stop swearing at couriers and instead come up with solutions. That small problem created a habit of noticing, and turned my profanities into opportunities for creativity. I'm not the only one to lean into cursing.

Like many of the best ideas, it started down the pub. Three friends met in the Pipe & Slippers in Bristol to complain about their jobs over a pint or two. As is so often the way, they shared dreams of having an idea that would make them millions. If others could do it, why not them? Between them they had lots of brilliant experience and complementary skills. They should do it.

Unlike many plans dreamt up over a pint or two (or three or four), they made theirs happen. The next month Jeremy Greaves, Mark Dale and Will Bolt booked a meeting room and sat down to pitch ideas to each other. It was fun, but something was missing – they realised that the best ideas don't happen in a vacuum. Greaves explains:

> 'We were looking at it the wrong way. We realised that the way you need to start is to think about all the times in your life where you go, "Oh, for fuck's sake, that doesn't work" or, "This is no good" or, "I wish there was a product that helped me do this" or, "I wish there was something that stopped this thing happening in my life."'

The FFS Club was born.

The friends found their mission – whenever they came across a 'for fuck's sake' situation, that's where true innovation would be found. They thought about all the problems they had in their lives, from annoying software to tripping over on the pavement to not being able to clean a toilet properly.

'We're going to find a solution to a problem that exists, where a solution isn't there yet,' says Greaves. 'Once we went and looked at it like that, it really helped us come up with some really good ideas.'

The club now meets once a month for two to three hours. Rather than rely on their own experience, they invite guests who share their FFS moments and provide diverse problems to evaluate. They meet in one of their workplaces and use a room with all the works – whiteboard, computers, a projector. They have a process for evaluating the problems and taking them forward to market – this is important as it forces them to assess viability of ideas at an early stage and reject ones that won't work. (More on this to come.) After a session they keep true to their roots and head back to the pub for a pint.

As Greaves says, the FFS Club 'is honest, it's fun, it's not scary, there's no bullshit'. And most importantly, it's working. With several ideas in development the friends pool their shared experience and expertise, work with others, and take forward solutions to problems that didn't previously exist.

PICK PROBLEMS THAT MATTER – TO YOU

In the early 2000s Anurag Acharya was working for Google. He was part of a small team building the web search index. The company was growing fast and the work was intense. 'I was burnt out,' says Acharya. 'So, I took a break, a sabbatical of sorts.' Along with his colleague Alex Verstak, the pair started work on a side project. Together they invented Google Scholar, a search engine that indexes scholarly and legal information, enabling anyone, anywhere in the world, to find academic articles.

It solved a problem Acharya had encountered many years ago. Studying in pre-internet days, Acharya had limited access to scholarly articles – if he wanted to read an article, he had to write a letter requesting a copy of the original article. This tactic worked around half the time, with hard copy reprints being sent to him by post. As a student at India's Institute of Technology, he was deprived of knowledge because of difficulties distributing the latest research information. This was the problem he was destined to solve.

At Google, he was determined to improve access to scholarly information in web search. The issue had changed; instead of the scarcity he experienced as a student, the new problem was that a search query returned *everything* when people typed a term into a browser. It was information overload. Acharya explains:

> 'The challenge is that for web search you have to guess whether the user wants scholarly results or more layperson results. As a first step to working on this, we said: "What if we didn't have to solve this problem? What could we do if we knew the user wanted scholarly results?"'

Google gave him the opportunity and resources to figure this out. Acharya and Verstak worked with scholarly publishers to build a new web search and, after a few months, they had a demo.

Acharya says: 'Google provided all that we needed, and asked for, to build Scholar – machines as well as the time for Alex and me to work on it full-time. Once we had a demo, many of our colleagues used it and gave us feedback.'

One of the colleagues who saw the demo was Google co-founder Larry Page. His reaction was to say: 'Why is this not live yet?' [9]

Google Scholar was born. With the support of his employer, Acharya could solve a problem he'd been puzzling over for decades. Acharya advises us to 'pick problems that matter. Something that, if you were wildly successful, would make a difference.' That's exactly what you'll do now.

CHOOSING THE BEST PROBLEM

Which problem matters most to you? It might be the one you feel most strongly about; it could make you angry, excited or super curious to find out more.

Which problem gives you an itch you want to scratch? There's no right or wrong answer here.

It's your idea you'll be creating. Only you can choose. Don't force it. Enjoy the time you spend. Trust your instincts and forget what other people might say.

Can't decide which one is best?

Evaluate each one: score them out of ten, type them into a spreadsheet, write them on Post-it notes and rank them, or let your lucky snail loose and pick the one it stops on.

You'll know when you find it.

And if there are several contenders, that's fantastic – you have a pipeline to work on and you can give Elon Musk a run for his money in the serial entrepreneur stakes.

Go for the one that interests you most now. File the others away – they'll be waiting for you when you're ready to solve them.

How to choose between problems

Decisions, decisions. It's easy to get overfaced when you've got lots of options. If you can't decide, follow these tips to get unstuck:

1. Don't stress about it. Enjoy the process. Ease the pressure off.

2. Read through your problems.

3. Highlight all the ones that make you feel excited.

4. Cross off the ones which make you feel a bit 'meh' – wave goodbye to boring.

5. Identify two or three criteria for judging against, think of your own or pick from: access, ease, motivation, size of problem or size of market, your own knowledge, and the all-important tingle factor – what will fulfil your dreams of a lifestyle or business opportunity.

6. Put the problems in a grid and score against your criteria using a one- to five-star system.

7. Tally up the results and see which scores the highest.

8. Finally, trust your gut. You'll know if it's the right one.

WRITE A PROBLEM STATEMENT

As Charles Kettering, inventor of the electric refrigerator and air conditioner, said: 'a problem well-stated is half-solved.'

Now you've got your problem, let's halve your work by writing what innovation experts call a 'problem statement'. It describes the challenge you aim to solve in an easy to understand sentence.

It might take a few attempts to write one, especially if you're a perfectionist, or are working with other people as you all need to agree the same problem. Here are some ideas to help you nail it:

- Grab a piece of paper or, if you're working with other people, a sheet of flip chart paper.

- Write a first attempt in the centre of the page with lots of white space around it. Just get it down – the point is to improve it, not start with a perfect version.

- Look at the sentence and ask if you understand what each word means. For example, when you say 'people' do you mean people of a certain age, gender, location? Be precise.

- Edit, scribbling out words, trying other ones, until you've found a version that works for you.

- If you're working in a group, you'll know you've got it right when you all agree. This might take some time!

- Write out the final sentence in best. High five (optional).

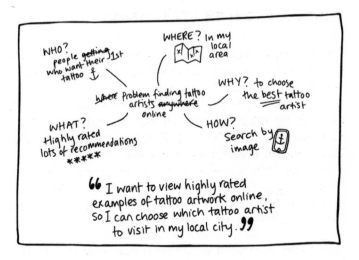

A STUDENT OF PROBLEMS HONES HER STATEMENT

Nicole Raby, a third-year undergraduate student of biology with enterprise at Leeds University, was tasked with generating business ideas for her final project. She hunted problems and generated a list of potential candidates, starting with her bugbear of finding petite gym wear, to developing diverse makeup and skincare ranges personalised for skin type, and countering the frustration of comparing beauty products online, before landing on one that got her excited.

When students first go to university, they encounter a new world of opportunity – things to do, people to meet, places to go. It's all a bit overwhelming, and the fear of missing out can be crushing, imagining that everyone else is having the time of their life while you struggle to figure out what's going on.

Raby experienced this problem herself, and as each new intake of freshers arrived, she saw it reflected in their eager young faces.

With so much going on, and so little time, how can students figure out where to go to make the most of their university experience?

That sentence outlines the problem in broad terms, but to create a great problem statement takes a little more precision. For example, when Raby talks about students – who exactly? Is it all students, first-years, or just freshers in their first few days? What about the phrase 'where to go' – is it in the town or city, or just on campus? And how about 'make the most of' – what does that mean? What are the benefits they might feel, the gains they might make when they find somewhere to go?

By asking the five Ws – Who, What, Where, When, Why – and the sixth question, How, you'll get to the bottom of the problem and be able to define what you mean. To refine Raby's problem, it becomes: *As a fresher I want to find out what events are going on in my university campus so I can go along and meet people, make friends and have new experiences.*

GET CURIOUS AND GET MOVING

Let's go back to Jo Caley, standing in her bedroom holding a ripped pair of jeans. Her anger turned to interest when she discovered the problem of vanity sizing that affects millions of women. A self-proclaimed geek, she went digging for data, and it soon snowballed. Like Caley, you'll need to stay curious.

Over the next few chapters we'll follow Caley and other startup founders who discovered problems at school, at work and on holiday. We'll get advice from experts on how to turn those problems into solutions, generate ideas, and choose the best that you can build and share with the world.

Grab your problem by the hand and get moving – the journey has just begun.

CHAPTER SUMMARY

- **In short**: Starting with a problem is the best way to have an idea.

- **Start now**: Write a list of problems, as many as you can possibly find or remember.

- **Go expert**: Make a habit of gathering problems, keep a problem notebook, or create a FFS club.

- **Be happy**: Being curious is fun – find your weird and enjoy getting out of your comfort zone.

- **Next step**: Gain a deeper understanding by finding out who else has your problem.

CHAPTER TWO

People

Fresh out of med school, Dr Mohammad Al-Ubaydli landed his first rotation working in a hospital. The non-medical world was becoming increasingly digital, and clinical staff were getting left behind. Because of his experience in software development, he was given the task of getting the other doctors to use personal, hand-held computers called Palm Pilots. But they didn't want to – the doctors had enough on their plates saving lives. He was stuck. How could he get them to see that this was an important issue alongside everything else they had to contend with? Even his own supervisor was reluctant to engage with this.

'The consultant surgeon I worked for – I couldn't get him to talk about Palm Pilots,' says Dr Al-Ubaydli. So instead, he got the surgeon to talk about the things that mattered to him. Why?

'Empathy,' says David Kelley, founder of the d.school and IDEO, 'is a gateway to the better and sometimes surprising insights that can help distinguish your idea or approach.'

When the surgeon opened up about his interests, he talked about golf. That gave Dr Al-Ubaydli an idea. He explains: 'So I said, "I'll write some Palm Pilot software to track your golf scores." He loved it, and he introduced me to everyone, saying, "You have to get this person to write you software."'

Dr Al-Ubaydli had figured out that to get people's attention you had to find out what they want and need. Soon he was working with the medical staff and writing medical software. He stopped seeing it in his own terms and instead saw it from other people's perspective, working out what their problems were, and then how he could help. What's more, it was fun and he made friends.

'It's a real pleasure to work with people like that. Somebody would tell me the problem, I fixed it that night trying to write the software, and the next day we tried it on the ward round. It was such good fun – you could see the effect on the patient care on the wards.'

If you're creating something, you need to understand that you are not your audience. There may be similarities, but your problem and pains, your likes and dislikes, needs and wants, attitudes and behaviours will all differ from other people's.

START WITH PEOPLE

In the narrative of creative success, this is how ideas happen: solitary genius is struck by inspiration, has groundbreaking idea, makes something, people love it, huge success, happy ever after. Research has quashed that myth. Creativity and innovation can be taught so that anyone, and everyone, can have ideas – we just need to get started.

In the last chapter we looked at how the best way to come up with an idea is to start with a problem, ideally one you experience yourself. At Stanford's d.school, they advise starting elsewhere: 'In design thinking we always say: "Don't start with the problem, start with the people, start with empathy."'[10]

This is especially helpful if you struggled to come up with a problem or if you're worried that the problem you found is something only you experience. By talking to other people you'll find out what their experience is, and this will transform your understanding of the problem, introduce you to new and more exciting problems, and help you find better solutions.

Dr Al-Ubaydli's whole career put that lesson into practice: he listened to people as he designed and built Patients Know Best – medical records owned and controlled by the patient. Dr Al-Ubaydli started with his own experience of having a rare genetic immune disorder; that insight gave him empathy with his first users who were looking after people with rare disorders.

He learnt that you must first understand people before you create solutions for them – whether they are a golf-playing senior surgeon, a medical colleague or other people with rare conditions.

'You have to sit with the users in the front line,' says Dr Al-Ubaydli. 'They'll tell you things that you cannot get from the computer logs, and they love it when you come back the next week and say: "Look I fixed what you said."'

We'll find out about how to involve your audience in testing and building your idea later in the book, but first, let's go and meet some people.

In this chapter you will:

- Move beyond your own experience by creating personas.

- Learn how to talk to people to find out their problems.

- Observe people in action to figure out what's really going on.

- Make sense of the pain with an empathy map.

IS IT JUST ME?

If you don't speak to people you won't know if you're the only one with a problem, or if there's a bigger and better problem waiting to be uncovered. It all starts with listening.

For a while I worked in a writers' centre. In between the workshops the writers would gather in the kitchen to make a brew – it was the perfect place to indulge my fascination with writing. I struggled to find the time to write regularly, so it felt natural to chat to people about how and when they wrote. I found out that pretty much every writer has a problem with procrastination, busyness and scheduling time to write. Those conversations led me to develop Prolifiko, a productivity coach for writers.

Listening to people kick-started my startup. Other people's problems are fascinating, and it's fun talking to new people and finding things out. Not that I always felt that way. I remember my teenage mortification at having to stop shoppers at a local supermarket as part of a school study trip. I hid my blushes behind a clipboard, ran through the survey questions as quickly as possible, and made up most of the answers. I imagine my research subjects found it as excruciating as I did.

As I got older, I learnt that people love talking about what's important to them – and I loved asking them questions.

If you've already got a problem in mind, think about who else might share it. Or perhaps there's a group of people you'd like to build something for – a target market. Before you go out and talk to them, let's gather together what you already know about them. A great way to focus on other people is to create a persona.

CREATE A PERSONA

If you want your creations, products and services to be used by real people you need to understand who they are and where you can find them. That's where personas can help. A persona isn't a real person, but a fictional, generalised version to keep your potential users in mind.

I visited a games design studio where the team was made up of single, male coders straight out of university. The audience for their games was 40-something women with children. To help them understand their audience they used a persona called 'Barbara'. Whenever they were planning new features or prioritising their development roadmap they would ask, 'Would Barbara like it?' That meant celebratory gun fire and explosions were replaced by champagne and confetti. 'Barbara' loved it and engagement shot up – like a firework rather than a missile.

You can also use personas for generating ideas – having a concrete example of who you're solving a problem for unlocks not just creativity but creates a sense of purpose and mission.

There isn't a strict checklist of sections, but personas typically include a picture, a name and demographics. They're presented on one page so you can see at a glance the key characteristics – also handy to pin up over your desk, save in your ideas folder, or share on slides or posters. The expert ones are created from market research, but at this stage, you're going to create a quick and dirty persona based on assumptions so you can get moving fast.

To create a persona, grab a large piece of paper and divide into four sections:

1. Name

2. Facts – such as biographical, demographic details

3. Behaviours – what they do

4. Needs and goals – what they want

Fill in the sections with your best guess about people who have your problem, or the audience you're trying to understand more about. You can get creative as you build up a sketch of someone. Think about:

- Demographics including age, gender, location, education and family.

- Occupation and how they spend their 'working' time – if they are freelance, student, work from home. Or if they have a job, their title, role details, the sort of company they work for and their salary.

- Hobbies, media preferences, technology, how they spend their spare time.

- Values – what they believe in and how important that belief is in their life.

- Needs – what they want, their goals and what challenges stop them achieving their goals – list any fears and worries.

If you want to add in further details, hit the internet to check social media profiles and online forums. There's a huge amount of detail publicly available and there's no need to be creepy – just search online for free profiling tools.

Finish by coming up with a name and perhaps drawing a sketch of the person, or getting a licence-free or stock photo online. The idea is to make them feel alive so you know exactly who your persona is.

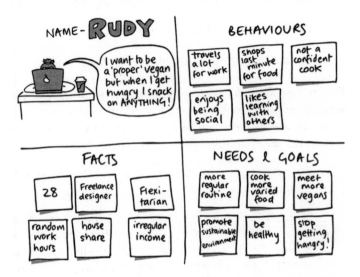

In the last chapter we met Nicole Raby, a third-year student at Leeds University who was working on her final year business project. She had identified a problem she'd experienced herself as a fresher wanting to find out what events were happening on campus. She knew other people felt the same sense of confusion, overload and fear of missing out. To help work out who they were, she drew up a persona.

At this stage, you're creating an assumption persona, which might be subject to your own bias and prejudice. Be mindful of this, but don't let it hold you back from the task. As you get to know your persona better you can update and counter your assumptions with facts. Empathy is a journey of understanding; it's important to start and then build on what you know as you learn about other people.

Once you've got a sense of your persona, it's time to go out and talk to them.

HOW TO TALK TO CUSTOMERS – THE AMAZON WAY

Over the past 25 years, Amazon has put innovation at the heart of its strategy. While its market-dominating disruption has many critics, there is much to learn from it. I got a sneak peek inside the innovation arm of Amazon and discovered its approach to 'things yet to be invented'.

It all starts with talking to potential customers, not to sell them something, but to listen. To get people to open up, you need to prepare questions, and the advice from Amazon is to keep it loose, think about three to five questions to hang a conversation around. This gives you freedom to follow interesting leads without the restriction of a rigid question structure.

One go-to opener is getting people to walk through their day. This means asking specific questions about their schedule and how they spend their time. My Amazon insider spoke about the 'Five Whys': where you ask a 'why' question and keep digging to find out what lies underneath people's automatic responses, actions and thought processes, such as why they chose a certain book to read.

Staff at Amazon are encouraged to get out and talk to customers. This is rare. Many companies only let trained researchers speak to customers, after all, interviewing is a specialist skill that can take years to hone, so it might make sense to leave it to the professionals. But, if staff don't engage with customers, they will become disconnected from the people they're making stuff for.

You need to keep connected to people as you build your idea. It's essential for you to talk to them and get feedback – how else will you know you're making something people want?

Build your confidence at this problem-finding stage by talking to people about their lives. Don't be scared. Ask people if you can talk to them, listen carefully to what they say, and afterwards make a note of what's important. With a bit of confidence and practice you'll be listening like a pro and gathering a tonne of valuable insight. Here are a few tried and tested approaches to get you started.

INTERVIEW TIPS

- Prepare a loose question structure, but don't stick slavishly to it.

- Make the questions open-ended so you don't get a series of 'yes' or 'no' answers. Instead of asking, 'Do you come here often?' ask, 'How often do you come here?'

- Ask naïve questions that get people to explain; a great starter is: 'Tell me about a time when you ...'

- Keep asking 'why' to probe further and unearth what people really think and do. But don't interrogate if you feel you're drilling too hard. An alternative approach is to ask: 'What else?'

- Listen – don't interrupt; instead leave pauses or quiet spaces to give people time to think and respond.

- Build rapport by listening, nodding and asking follow-up questions that show you're paying attention.

- Don't judge or dispute what they say; stay curious.

- Record their responses. Make notes or voice record, and when you are finished thank them for their time.

- As soon as possible afterwards, summarise key points from your notes about what struck you most.

TAKE IT UP A LEVEL: HOW TO OBSERVE PEOPLE'S PROBLEMS

Professional researchers don't just listen, they observe and record people. Think of it like anthropology, where you venture into the unchartered territories of people's lives – right here on your doorstep. It's a fascinating process, and if you're keen to expand your problem-hunting repertoire, read on.

Paul-Jervis Heath founded design agency Modern Human with the goal of designing products based on real human behaviour. The agency does this not by asking people what they want, but by observing what they do.

By uncovering people's behaviour, you get to understand their needs, goals, values and motivations, and only then can you develop products and services for them. This process is called 'design research'.

The first step is to see people in their natural environment, whether it's their office, home or somewhere else they spend their time.

Once you're there you observe. Heath's advice is to capture everything you're witnessing, even things that might not seem important in people's behaviour and body language. For example, what they say is less important than their tone of voice – are they angry, excited, happy or bored? Make notes, take photos or film them going about their daily tasks.

You'll get a sense of how they do things, their habits and routines. You might find workarounds, where people have hacked together solutions to overcome problems; these are worth paying attention to, because it means someone cares enough to design their own solution. You might also spot a mismatch between what people say and what they do.

Observations are a great starting point, but to ace design research you need to take it up a level and gather 'findings'. Heath explains:

> 'Observations are counting the things that you capture while you're out in the field, but findings are the patterns within those observations.'

You need to interpret what you saw to find patterns. Observe several people. Draw conclusions like 'Four out of five people do this'. Once you have patterns, you're on your way to uncovering 'insight', which is research gold.

An insight is a penetrating truth about people's aspirations or motivations that can be used to make a new product or service, or to make an existing one better.

Once you have true insight you can unlock solutions. We'll come to that in the next chapter.

HOW TO BECOME A TOP RESEARCHER

Boost your research skills by learning from the masters of observation with these expert tips:

1. Ask people if you can observe them in their homes, offices or at leisure.

2. Get permission to record, take photos or film them.

3. Have an idea about what task you want to observe. For example, is it how they cook a meal, save photos from their phone, or choose an outfit to wear?

4. A good prompt to get them started is: 'Show me how you ...'

5. Get them to talk you through the process, explaining each step as they take it.

6. Keep curious and interested, and don't judge – check out the interview tips from earlier.

7. Notice their body language, tone of voice and any behaviour that shows how they're feeling.

8. Afterwards, make a record as quickly as possible while everything is fresh in your mind. The longer you leave it, the more likely you'll misremember and the subtleties will be lost.

9. Analyse your observations to find patterns and draw conclusions that lead to insight.

These are advanced qualitative research techniques, so start small to bag some quick wins. One tip is to identify the smallest possible task you wish to observe and see if you can find people doing it in a public area. Once you've got a few public observations under your belt, you can ask to observe people in their own environment. You only need a handful of people, say five to ten, and while it's best to avoid family and friends, do ask them for recommendations and introductions to people who fit your persona.

DESIGN RESEARCH IN ACTION

Heath worked on a project looking at people's attitudes to mortgages to discover what influences their decisions. When he spoke to people, they explained their rational grown-up approaches to money management.

In addition to interviewing them, Heath asked them to keep a diary tracking the process from when they decided to move house, all the way through choosing a mortgage and getting it approved.

When he compared the interviews with the diary studies, there was a huge difference between what people said in the interviews that they had done, and what they had actually done according to their diaries. Remember, these are the same people reporting the same experiences! He explains:

> 'The issue wasn't that they were lying to us. The issue was that they were lying to themselves. We all assume that we act rationally, but actually, when we write down what we're doing right now, at any moment in time, and then link those things together, you see that the things we do are not always rational at all.'

Design research gets closer to real human behaviour through techniques like observation and tracking. It helps you to understand people's goals and values as they are played out in reality, rather than in the stories people tell themselves.

EMPATHY – TAKING A WALK IN SOMEONE ELSE'S SHOES

One of the biggest assets you have in solving problems is empathy.

Empathy helps you to experience the feelings, thoughts or attitudes of others, using the power of your imagination. You identify with people, step into their shoes, and channel what they're going through. It's an innovation super power, and it takes time and effort, but if you figure out what people really need (rather than what they say they want) you can create amazing solutions.

Some design researchers take the concept of 'taking a walk in someone else's shoes' a little further; at design agency IDEO, founder David Kelley says:

> 'Our first-person experiences help us form personal connections with the people for whom we're innovating. We've washed other people's clothes by hand in their sinks, stayed as guests in housing projects, stood beside surgeons in operating rooms, and calmed agitated passengers in airport security lines – all to build empathy.'[11]

You don't need to go so far (although you can imagine how powerful it would be); if you've spoken to other people, asked them questions about their daily lives and the problems they face, perhaps observed them in their homes and offices, you'll have gathered a whole bunch of useful information. It might be a bit messy – notes scribbled on a notepad, voice recordings on your phone, photos or videos – so now's the time to make sense of it all. As Paul-Jervis Heath says, turn those observations into insights. A great tool for doing this is an empathy map.

EMPATHY MAPS FOR DEEPER UNDERSTANDING

'The most important person that you need to focus on when you're designing a product or service,' says Dave Gray, 'is the person who's going to use it.'

In short, if you start with the user in mind, you'll design a better solution.

Gray is the founder of XPLANE, a visual thinking company that helps people develop shared understanding to create lasting, sustainable impact through design. He created empathy maps, a practical tool for understanding people so we can create better products, services and experiences for them.

Empathy maps give you a deeper understanding of people, by making sense of the information you have and helping you to spot gaps in your findings. I find them to be most useful at this early stage before you've created a solution, so that you keep people in mind throughout the design and build process. Empathy maps become a touchstone and reality check as you develop your hustle.

It's a flexible exercise, takes about twenty minutes, and, although it was designed to be done in a group, it works perfectly if you're by yourself.

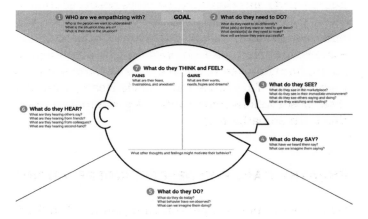

© 2017 Dave Gray, xplane.com[12]

First, get a copy of the map – you can find one online, but to get the latest version go to the Gamestorming website[13] – and draw or print it as large as you can, ideally on a flip chart sheet or A1 poster.

The next step is to populate the sections, starting at one, using the questions as prompts:

1. WHO are we empathising with?

2. What do they need to DO?

3. What do they SEE?

4. What do they SAY?

5. What do they DO?

6. What do they HEAR?

7. What do they THINK and FEEL? (What are their PAINS and GAINS?)

Section seven asks 'What do they think and feel?' and asks you to list them as 'pains' and 'gains'. This is about more than creating a neatly rhyming couplet – it helps you to home in on what's most important. Pains are pretty obvious: stuff that hurts enough to be a problem, like those frustrating moments when you're returning unwanted online orders and you have to wait in a queue at the post office during your lunch break. Gains are what you experience when the pain is removed – for example, the joy of getting to the post office and finding there is no queue, you get served immediately, get the return processed, and have time to treat yourself to a slap-up lunch with your soon-to-be refunded money. To understand someone's gains, think about what they hope to achieve, or what 'good' (or amazing) looks like to them.

You can make a guess about what people might say, but it is most valuable to use real quotes wherever possible. That's where all your notes from your interviews and observations will come in handy.

Rather than write directly onto the map, write quotes and observations on Post-it notes and stick them in the sections. This is helpful as you may want to move answers around and cluster them into themes, especially if there are several people working on a map together. You might have ten, twenty or even 30 in each section. Then, prioritise the top five. Debate is all part of the process, so allow time to discuss in a group, or question your own choices if you're working alone.

REFRAME THE PROBLEM – AS OTHERS SEE IT

In the last chapter, you wrote a problem statement based on you own experience. Now that you've gathered insights about other people, it's time to revisit and revise your problem statement with these new insights, or create a new one that starts with other people's problems.

Look over your empathy map: what problems have you identified? Often, the biggest problems are staring you right in the face under the 'pains' section, but also look at the gains, and how you can help people achieve their goals, and check out the other sections for those nuggets of insight gold.

As before, write your problem in the centre of a piece of paper, and edit, scribbling out words as you refine and focus down on what people really need.

FROM EMPATHY TO SOLUTIONS

Empathy mapping sets aside your own assumptions and puts other people's experiences first. I've used empathy maps in many ways – with project teams to collate research we've gathered, in workshops to kick off product development, and most powerfully working with end users themselves.

In one session, rather than use interviews, observations and insights, I got undergraduate students to fill in empathy maps to understand their own experiences. Working in teams, they collated their personal engagement with the world, talking about ways in which they differed and what they shared, until they created a rounded view of a 'second-year university student' – one they could all understand, appreciate and empathise with.

The students' biggest problems, listed as 'pains' within the empathy map, included: social isolation, negative social media, time management, writing a dissertation that made the most of their learning, getting lecturers to understand their needs and deliver better lectures, and making the most of opportunities while at university to build skills and relationships and find career fulfilment.

I was surprised and humbled by what they shared. They grappled with big problems and worked collaboratively to solve them. They used the maps as a prompt for developing solutions – which we'll do next. The teams developed different ideas which were entered into a pitch competition, and then they voted on the winning idea.

Although the idea with the most votes involved rewarding students with alcohol for meeting deadlines, the problems they were trying to solve were anything but frivolous. It helped me to understand the challenges they faced, and for the teams, they could discuss some of their biggest challenges in a safe environment, understand they weren't alone, listen to others, and work together to seek solutions. Everyone left that session feeling more empathy for one another.

Using the direct experience of people transforms not only how you see problems, but also how you create solutions. You'll involve your audience in testing and building your idea later in the book, but up next, we're going to generate some ideas.

CHAPTER SUMMARY

- **In short**: Listen to people to understand what problems they face.

- **Start now**: Draw an assumption persona so you can keep people in mind when you design your solution.

- **Go expert**: Make like an anthropologist and observe people in action to uncover insight into their lives.

- **Be happy**: Get in touch with your feelings and create an empathy map.

- **Next step**: Grab your new or updated problem statement – it's time to generate some solutions.

CHAPTER THREE

Solutions

When Charlotte Cramer walked past a homeless guy on the streets of Berlin one autumn day, she couldn't get him out of her head. She was on holiday with her friend Scarlett Montanaro:

> 'We were on our way to get a coffee when a homeless guy approached us and asked us for some spare change. Just as I'd always done, we shrugged him off and walked the other way, but we were left with this real feeling of guilt. How ridiculous it was, that not only had we not given him the one or two euros he was looking for, we'd then gone and spent six euros on a coffee. There was this dissonance between not doing something that was definitely accessible to you and feeling bad as a result of it.'

Homelessness, an increasing feature of our unequal society, is a complex problem to solve; it feels too overwhelming for us alone to tackle, so we ignore it and accept that it's the way things are. But for Cramer, it niggled. She kept going back to her personal feeling of unease. Mulling it over with Montanaro, they figured out that people worry about how the money will be spent, so what should be an act of charity – giving money to someone in need – makes us feel bad.

When Cramer returned to London, she was confronted by messages about homelessness, from posters saying that giving money to people on the street would contribute to their early death, to government facts and media myths. To find out what people really thought, she spoke to them, asking questions like: How often do you give to homeless people? Do you feel empathy towards homeless people? How do you feel when you see homeless people on your walk to work? Have you ever given to a charity that supports people who are homeless?

Now deep in research mode, Cramer and Montanaro talked to the experts. 'We went to shelters and soup kitchens,' says Cramer, 'and spoke to the people who worked there; we spoke to people who were currently affected by homelessness. We arranged a meeting with the CEO of *The Big Issue* who gave us a lot more insight into the realities of homelessness and the complexity of it.'

Speaking to people directly affected by homelessness led to a breakthrough.

FALL IN LOVE WITH THE PROBLEM

Pascal Finette tells it like it is. A serial entrepreneur, contributor to several high-growth startups, and mentor to founders, he's better known as the Heretic. His advice on building a successful company is to stop having 'crazy-ass ideas' and instead get curious.

Finette offers the example of Google, whose founders Larry Page and Sergey Brin 'started out in their college dorm solving a vexing problem they experienced firsthand – search.'[14]

This was the problem that floated their boat, not the grand ambition of organising the world's information.[15] Like the Google founders, Cramer had a problem that caught her interest and that she couldn't stop thinking about.

Finette says the most successful entrepreneurs he meets are 'insanely knowledgeable about the problem space they operate in. They rattle down all the relevant stats, know by heart where the discrepancies in the data are and have developed a deep understanding and empathy for their users. In a nutshell: They fell in love with the problem. And they usually did so way before they started thinking about the solution.'[16]

It was during the research phase that Cramer finally got a handle on the problem, and the words came straight from a homeless man. He told them: 'People don't give me money because they think it will be spent on crack and cider.'

'Off the back of that insight,' Cramer says, 'we set ourselves a brief, of how might we create the most simple and transparent model for charitable giving, where people know exactly what their money will be spent on.'

FINDING SOLUTIONS

That brief led to them setting up CRACK + CIDER, an online shop where customers can buy useful items for their city's homeless. The shop has the most essential items a homeless person might need, based on the advice of local shelters, and uses existing networks of shelters and soup kitchens to get the item purchased into the hands of those most in need.

The model works, with an average donation in the UK of £28, a sum much greater than the kind of loose change usually handed to someone begging on the streets.

You've got a problem you're curious about, you know who has the problem and what pain it causes them. Now you're going to come up with solutions. It's time to get creative, and:

- Start small to ease yourself into the right mindset.

- Find the phrase that will trigger your creative problem solving.

- Go divergent and draw some mind maps.

- Collaborate on a brainstorm.

MORE IDEAS LEAD TO BETTER SOLUTIONS

'The only way to have a good idea is to have lots of ideas,' said Linus Pauling, a creative polymath whose deep engagement in the world around him gave him great pleasure and success. An award-winning scientist, he's the only person to have won two unshared Nobel Prizes, which he bagged in two completely different categories, chemistry and peace.

Let's follow Pauling's advice that having more ideas leads to better solutions, and find out why quantity trumps quality at this stage of your hustle.

'Decision makers often jump on the first idea that comes along, and then spend years trying to make it work. This is a key cause of failure.'[17] Professor Paul Nutt has been studying bad decisions for over twenty years. Using data from over 400 business decisions, he found that two out of three decisions are failure prone. He found that failure is often caused by taking an 'idea-driven' process rather than one led by discovery. If you're wedded to a single idea, now's the time to come up with some alternatives.

Professor Nutt found a positive correlation between the number of ideas on offer and the ultimate success of the decision to work on that one idea. More ideas lead to better outcomes, significantly so. If you want to give your idea a better chance of success, you need to widen your ideas pool. He explains:

> 'Identify more than one option. Several competing options improve results. Discarded options are not wasted. They help you confirm the value of a preferred course of action and frequently offer ways to improve it.'[18]

In short, having several ideas on offer means you can compare them, and when you've picked one to work on, you'll be able to defend that choice. If you've started off with a single idea you'd like to work on, now's the time to come up with some alternatives. Nutt found that having two alternatives to the original idea led to success in two-thirds of the decisions he studied.

When you have lots of ideas, you have choices, which means you're more likely to find a good idea among the options available. Also, if you just have one idea, it's going to be really hard to give it up; if you have several, you're less likely to get attached to them, giving you more chance to back a winner. Finally, having lots of ideas gets us past the obvious answers, so we get to be more creative.

Imagine you're in a job interview and someone asks you to name the business person who inspires you the most. Your mind will quickly jump to recognisable names. We need to clear these obvious answers out of the way before we get to the really inspiring people, the ones about whom we can tell a story that impresses the interviewer. While Richard Branson might be the obvious choice, saying he inspires you isn't going to reveal anything interesting about you. Instead, think of five or ten people, and somewhere down the bottom of that list you'll find a more creative and unique answer to the question. Congratulations – you've got the job.

DIVERGENT THINKING

Coming up with lots of ideas is an example of divergent thinking. This type of creativity takes an indirect route to problem solving, by analysing the problem and generating many possible ideas to reach a solution. It's associated with creative types like designers and those working in innovation.

Convergent thinking is the opposite – it involves honing in on a correct answer, often as quickly as possible. It's the sort of thinking we're taught at school and is necessary to pass exams in a traditional setting. Think of a historian reciting dates, names and events.

The difference can be illustrated by these two exercises. For convergent thinking, the exercise is to think of a word that rhymes with 'goat'. For divergent thinking, you'd instead aim to come up with as many words you can think of that rhyme with 'goat'.

When you're thinking of solutions, you need to diverge and come up with lots of ideas. Film-maker David Lynch likens it to fishing:

'If you get an idea that's thrilling to you, put your attention on it and these other fish will swim into it. It's like a bait. They'll hook on to it and you'll get more ideas. And you just pull them in.'[19]

Coming up with ideas gets easier the more you do it – and the more ideas you have. Creative thinking is like a muscle: it can be trained, exercised and improved – and most importantly anyone can do it.

MRI scanners have transformed research into the neuroscience of creativity. Researchers have found that there is no one part of the brain responsible for creativity, but that highly creative people are able to engage large-scale brain networks.[20] The brain builds new networks and connections – a process known as neuroplasticity – so that we can change, learn new things, develop new habits and break old ones, and strengthen our problem-solving ability. It just takes a bit of exercise.

Creativity is our ability to think in new and original ways. A quick exercise you can do is to grab a regular household item, like an egg box, milk carton or toothbrush, and write a list of as many ways to use that item as you can think of.

Let's say we picked a condom as our item. The first uses would be the ones it was designed for, to prevent pregnancy and protect against sexually transmitted infections, but you could come up with other more original uses, such as carrying water. Many survivalists recommend keeping a condom in an emergency kit, not because come the apocalypse they're worried about STDs, but because of the many practical, life-saving uses they have – from starting fires, to using one as a slingshot or waterproof glove, to blowing one up like a balloon and painting a face on it to create a companion to combat loneliness. Now that's creative problem solving.

GETTING COMFORTABLE WITH CREATIVITY

While Jenn Maer thrives in a hotbed of creativity as senior design director at IDEO, her challenge is to engage clients who spend their days in front of Excel spreadsheets. She explains the importance of divergent thinking and going wide in the creative process:

> 'Divergence is not the straightest path to a solution. You need to explore in order to come up with new ideas. If you're just looking at the thing that you're trying to improve, you're never going to see what's outside that you could combine in a new way to create something, or find inspiration, or even give your brain the latitude to relax enough to let an idea come through.'

Divergence can make people feel uncomfortable, because they can't see what's happening, and it's hard to measure progress and value for money. Maer has an example of taking a client on a research day in New York City. To the client it looked like they were spending a whole day hanging around wasting time – but to the team it was a necessary part of the creative process of exploring and going wide. Although a lot of what they found was later discarded, they landed on a couple of pivotal findings. 'You can't get to that 20 per cent,' says Maer, 'without the other 80 per cent, because you don't know where the 20 per cent is going to be.'

That's the difference between a creative solution and an obvious one, and why IDEO and its methods have led to so many groundbreaking ideas, such as designing the first mouse for Steve Jobs' new computer back in 1980, or creating a whole new school system for Peru in 2015 including the buildings, teacher training, financial model and curriculum.[21]

CREATIVE PROBLEM SOLVING – THE SMALL APPROACH

It not just clients who fear the creative process. As individuals, many of us struggle to get our heads around divergence. Sometimes that discomfort stops us from ever getting started. Doing new things triggers the fear centres of the brain – the amygdala, often called the 'chimp brain' because of its primal response, such as overreacting when it senses potential threats. Although neuroplasticity means our brains can change, the amygdala prefers it when things are the same – routine is good because it protects us and keeps us safe. That's why it can be so hard to learn new habits: it takes up brain energy, which the amygdala would rather conserve for survival in case of emergency.

If you take on a project which is too big, for example solving world poverty, you risk setting off the alarm bells in the amygdala – and that's when fear and stress can overwhelm you. Once triggered, your amygdala takes a long time to calm down.

There are ways to get creative and start doing things outside of your comfort zone that won't trigger the fear centre. It starts by taking tiny steps. When steps are super-small and change is incremental then the amygdala doesn't notice when you crank up the time or effort. Here are some things to try:

- **Short sessions**. Set a timer for just five minutes and do a simple task such as writing some ideas and observations in a notebook. Actually, just open your notebook – no need to come up with ideas yet – make it so easy that not doing it isn't an option.

- **Do it in the morning**. Research has shown that many creative thinkers like writers and artists work best in the mornings. It's a combination of having a well-rested brain and fewer distractions.

- **Treat yourself**. Associating tasks with rewards is one of the surest routes to build a new habit, so get a nice coffee, grab some cake and get creative.

- **Lower the stakes**. Honestly, what will happen if you spend five minutes playing around with ideas? Make the task so small you can't fail.

- **Make it fun and enjoyable**. This could be anything from buying a nice notepad to visiting a creative place like an art gallery.

- **Use prompts**. There are so many creative triggers out there, a quick search will reveal a multitude. Try Oblique Strategies, invented by Brian Eno and Peter Schmidt in 1975; it has been triggering creativity for a lifetime.

Let's get cracking with a super simple, tried and tested approach for triggering creative problem solving.

KICK-START YOUR IDEAS BY FRAMING THE PROBLEM

The next exercise was called 'the secret phrase that top innovators use' by the *Harvard Business Review*.[22] We've already come across this phrase.

At the beginning of the chapter we found Charlotte Cramer feeling guilty about not giving money to a homeless person. Her bad feelings led her to explore what was going on: why people want to give charitably and what holds them back. After speaking to friends and family, those working in the sector, and people affected by homelessness, she found the insight that people worry about how their money will be spent, and that giving might lead to drink and drug-taking that could further harm someone. She said: 'Off the back of that insight, we set ourselves a brief, of *how might we ...*'

Those are the three magic words: How might we?

That combination of words opens us up to creative problem solving, by framing the question:

- 'How' creates an open question that prompts higher-order thinking and stimulates creativity.

- 'Might' suggests possibility, the opportunity for a solution to be discovered.

- 'We' means we'll do this together – by working with others, we combine our strengths and leverage our diversity to figure this thing out.

By writing your problem using the 'How might we ...?' format, you're using a framework that has been tried and tested by some of the most innovative companies, like IDEO,[23] Google and Facebook.

The simplest instruction to get going is to take your problem and rewrite it starting the sentence with the words: How might we ...

However, you need to be careful that the question is neither too broad nor too narrow. The best way to combat this is to write several options and pick the one that gives you the tingle of excitement and opportunity, balanced with being achievable.

Let's take Nicole Raby's problem of freshers finding events to go to. Asking, 'How might we find the best events in the world tonight?' will overwhelm us, but asking, 'How might we find events going on in our university campus right now?' will be too narrow. There will be a sweet spot of opportunity that acts as a launch pad for your creativity.

Write your problem in the 'How might we ...?' format and give it the once over. Check:

- Does it give you a little tingle of excitement? Feeling emotionally engaged and stimulated will make working on it more enjoyable and more likely that you keep going.

- Do you care about figuring this out? The more something matters, the higher the stakes and more likely you are to continue working on a hard problem.

- Is it broad enough to stimulate several solutions? There needs to be opportunity; otherwise, it's a simple closed question with just a few obvious answers.

- Do you feel overwhelmed by it? You won't be able to solve climate change in one brainstorm, so break down the problem into something smaller and more realistic.

You are the right person for this. Think about your personal experience of a problem and bring the richness of your life, opinions, skills, empathy and imagination to solve it.

FINDING THE RIGHT SIZED PROBLEM

Cramer and her co-founder Montanaro used the 'how might we' format to stimulate ideas, and one of their solutions was CRACK + CIDER. In Chapter 7 we'll find out how they built and tested their idea, but now, let's learn from their approach to problem solving.

'It's essential that you start by identifying and understanding exactly what the problem is that you're solving,' says Cramer. 'From the outside, it might look as though the problem we're solving is the issue of homelessness, or maybe you might think we're solving the issue of people who suffer from homelessness not having access to essential items. In fact, it wasn't any of those things.'

She explained that the problem they were solving was that people weren't giving money to people on the street even though they wanted to. Those conflicted feelings and sense of guilt were something she experienced first-hand. She was solving her own problem, which she admits feels a bit self-serving, but it was achievable. 'It's kind of embarrassing,' Cramer says, 'that it was our problem that we were solving rather than the problem that people who suffer from homelessness face, but sometimes that's the best way to make change happen.'

Although homelessness is a huge, complicated problem they found a way they could contribute. And they have made a huge difference to thousands of people's lives. Cramer adds: 'The fact that we came face to face with that problem personally every single day, that it was something that we were personally afflicted by, meant that we maintained the motivation and the excitement to address it.'

They engaged their 'seeking system' and found the right-sized problem: big enough to be challenging, small enough to know they could make a dent in it. It felt exciting, possible and something they had first-hand experience of.

WORKING ALONE: TRIGGER CREATIVE THINKING WITH MIND MAPS

Researchers have found that bypassing the conscious part of the mind boosts divergent thinking and leads to more creative ideas.[24] One technique that takes advantage of this approach is mind mapping.[25] It's a great approach to use if you are working by yourself.

Mind maps trigger the creative thinking needed for problem solving. They use free association to organise information graphically and create connections between words and concepts.

At its simplest, a mind map is a spider diagram, where words radiate out from a central concept using interlinking branches. By writing and drawing freely, you bypass the logic-driven part of your brain, quieten your inner critic and allow yourself to be creative. It quickly gets you unstuck, gets ideas flowing, and you can do it without any special tools – all you need is some blank paper and coloured pens.

To get started, use the largest sheet of paper you can find, turn it landscape, and aim to fill as much of it as you can.

1. A problem is the perfect launch pad for ideas, so write yours in the centre of the sheet and draw a circle around it.

2. Working around it, write down four or five related things you can think of. Don't judge or edit – just write whatever bubbles up. Draw circles around the words.

3. Use the words in the secondary circles as prompts to free-associate new thoughts. Aim for a single word each time – you're not looking for fully-formed ideas at this stage, just triggering new connections.

4. Draw lines linking your words together. The ideas at the outer level don't need to be directly linked to the central problem; you're following paths that are sparked from it, but not directly related.

5. Pro tip: use multiple colours, words and images, and make the lines curved rather than straight

and of different thicknesses to indicate strength of connection.

See the following example, where someone is looking at the problem of how to cut down their meat intake. At this stage they are exploring the issue, what connections can be made and what thoughts and ideas bubble up.

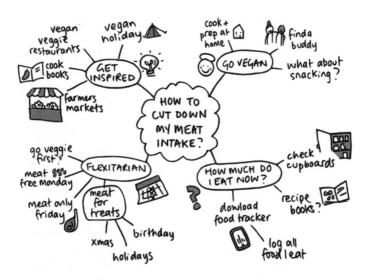

It might look a bit of a mess when you start but, as with any skill, you'll get better as you develop your own personal style of mind mapping. Keep it as graphic as possible, with space for lots of ideas and connections.

Review your mind map – what themes have emerged? Any new, interesting or original thoughts? Think how you can build on them – perhaps start a new mind map, with that new thought as your central concept to prompt new connections.

WORKING WITH OTHERS: COLLABORATIVE CREATIVE THINKING

'It's hard to be the only panda in the zoo,' Jenn Maer says. 'You need your people.'

Maer found her people at IDEO, the global design agency that champions design thinking, a human-centred approach to innovation. IDEO's success is down to its people; it's not about individual stars but collaboration. Maer describes it like being in a sports team where a sense of shared responsibility and confidence that someone has your back makes the team stronger. It also makes the ideas stronger:

> 'When I worked in advertising, it was very much a lone wolf kind of thing. You're in it for yourself and you're trying to get your ideas at the top. At IDEO, you're building on the ideas of other people and relying on their expertise – you can never tell where an idea came from by the time you get it out the door.'

Maer works with teams to create positive impact, solving problems with clients by designing better products, services and experiences. Brainstorming is central to how teams generate ideas. To be a good brainstormer takes practice, experience and structure.

'If you just sit in a room trying to bang out ideas, that's really hard,' says Maer, 'but if you add structure to it, a brainstorm can be magic.'

HOW TO BRAINSTORM

Brainstorms get a bad rap, often because people don't know how to do it properly. I can't be the only person who's had a senior manager demand new ideas on the spot, usually standing at the head of a long conference table and pointing aggressively at a whiteboard, shouting, 'Now, goddamnit, we're not leaving this room until we've come up with some new products.'

Working with other people can be serious fun. Whether you're organising a brainstorm at work or inviting mates round at the weekend, here's a five-step process to get the most from creative collaboration.

1. Pre-play: planning a brainstorm

- Be specific. Have something to brainstorm about. Sounds obvious, but you need to have a good question, problem statement or a 'How might we ...?' Creativity is a response, so focus on what will trigger imaginative thinking.

- Mix it up. You don't want a room full of the same types of people because you'll get the same ideas. Be as diverse as you can, on as many fronts as you can. Hunt down people with different backgrounds, opinions, jobs and experiences as well as people who consider themselves not to be creative.

- Keep a lid on numbers. You want enough people to spark ideas, but not so many it's a logistical nightmare. I'd invite six to twelve people for a tightly run, timed session of up to an hour.

2. Warming up: getting the session going

- Facilitate. Running an effective brainstorm takes a good facilitator. It's their job to explain the rules, get things started and keep it moving while keeping everyone inspired and engaged.

- Warm up. There is no optimal time to fit a brainstorm into a day. You're asking people to make time in a busy schedule and come from other meetings or jobs to contribute, leaving behind their overloaded inboxes, stresses and to-do lists. Welcome people, put them at ease, tell them what's happening and how long it will take, and then kick off with a quick and fun brainstorm to warm their creative muscles.[26]

- Increase energy. You want a fast-paced, creative session and, while it's great to have natural energy and laughter, sometimes some artificial stimulation is required. A spot of sugar goes a long way – so grab some sweets, cookies or fruit and nuts to fuel the ideas. Caffeine is cool, but alcohol is a no-no.

3. The main game: coming up with ideas

- Have rules. Creativity is not a free-for-all, anything goes situation; you need rules so that people feel safe and trusted, and to counteract any vulnerability they might feel in sharing ideas. The rules I swear by are:

    - Go for quantity not quality.

    - If you think it, share it – all ideas are good.

    - Defer judgement of your own and other people's ideas.

    - Build on each other's ideas – push ideas further.

- Go wild. If you start with a good question, people will stay on topic, but you need to push people to have creative, original and wild responses. If you've got the right environment they will feel safe to share their ideas.

- Work individually at first. Give everyone their own pen and stack of Post-it notes. Get them to write down their ideas – one per Post-it note. If I'm facilitating, I have a timed session of five to ten minutes to get people to write down their ideas before sharing. This stops extroverts (or senior managers) taking over.

4. Going public: sharing and building the ideas

- Share and cluster. Get someone to share a first idea by reading what's on a Post-it note. Stick it on the wall, and get similar ideas out. Cluster them together. It can get a bit messy, but a good facilitator will allow everyone to speak, read their ideas, generate new clusters, and stop people judging and shouting down ideas.

- Build. As ideas are shared they will spark off new connections and ideas. This is exactly what you want, getting people to say 'Yes, and ...' Encourage people to write these new ideas down so they are captured and can trigger other, better, wilder ideas.

- Organise. You'll have a wonderfully colourful wall of notes. Get the group to consider the clusters – if they are too big, make smaller clusters. Look for themes and label them, giving similar ideas names. A good facilitator will check in with the group, ask questions and encourage comment. Some people number the ideas – in a very creative session you might expect 100 ideas.

5. **Wrapping up: making decisions**

- Decide. The final part of the session wraps up with a decision and clear next steps. We'll talk about how to make decisions in the next chapter, but there should be a structure to help people to decide: some criteria and a way of voting that avoids group think and deference to the opinion of the most powerful person.

PASSIONATE ABOUT PROBLEM SOLVING

Charlotte Cramer had never been homeless, nor did she know anyone who was, but her experience of walking past someone begging on the street gave her a personal insight into homelessness. She took that experience and used it as a way into the problem, one she grew determined to solve.

'You have to be passionate about solving that problem rather than the solution,' Cramer says. 'The solution might have to change; it will always shift – there will be bureaucracy and complexities and money issues, and all the hurdles that you can possibly imagine, but if you are still passionate about the problem, then you'll have the enthusiasm and the excitement to keep going.'

Cramer along with her friend and co-founder Scarlett Montanaro got passionate about the problem. The more they looked into it, the more curious they got, and the more determined. They did their research, spent time with those affected by homelessness, and used that knowledge to generate solutions, which they tested. Not everything worked, and they faced many hurdles as they built CRACK + CIDER, an online shop that uses donations to provide essential items to those living on the streets.

By falling in love with the problem Cramer and Montanaro were motivated to continue, and so can you. Now you've got ideas, the next stage is to choose which one will best solve the problem.

CHAPTER SUMMARY

- **In short**: To find a good solution you need to have lots of ideas.

- **Start now**: Write a 'How might we ...?' question and draw a mind map to stimulate your creative thinking.

- **Go expert**: Collaborate to super-charge your problem-solving powers by organising a brainstorm with friends and colleagues.

- **Be happy**: Overcome your creative fear by starting small and keep some treats at hand.

- **Next step**: Gather up all your ideas – it's time to decide which one has legs.

CHAPTER FOUR

Choose

What makes a joke funny? Ira Glass of *This American Life* visited satirical local newspaper, *The Onion,* to investigate how it has created consistently funny fake news stories for 30 years. With millions of visitors to the website each month, every joke needs to land. Glass found the secret to comedy success lies in the Tough Room, the weekly editorial meeting.[27]

Every Monday the eight writers assemble. Each clutches a list of headlines, and they take turns pitching them. This consists of simply reading the headlines out one by one, with no argument or supporting evidence, just the headline. If two other people like the headline, it survives until the next round. Laughs are rare.

'It takes them two long mornings,' says Glass, 'on Monday and on Tuesday, to come up with these sixteen headlines they're going to use in the paper this week. And to get to those sixteen, they go through – and I know this number is going to sound kind of crazy – 600 possible headlines.'

QUANTITY THEN QUALITY

In the last chapter, Nobel Prize-winning scientist Linus Pauling championed the importance of generating lots of ideas. Quantity is the first principle of creative problem solving. However, there's a second part to his quote to consider:

> 'If you want to have good ideas you must have many ideas. Most of them will be wrong, and what you have to learn is which ones to throw away.'

The Onion's editorial process, tested over decades, has honed these two principles into a comedy machine. But getting your ideas rejected hurts; writer Megan Ganz described how her heart was still attached to her headlines and how, when they didn't make the cut, all her hard work evaporated into nothing. She gave Glass an example:

> 'I had this one that was, "Spork used as knife." And for some reason that was the funniest thing I'd ever thought of, the fact that here's a utensil that's two utensils, and you're using it as the only utensil it isn't. And it didn't even get a titter in the meeting. Nothing. It just died. And I read it twice, and they were like, "Yeah, move on." It was months ago that I wrote that headline. I still think about it.'

It wasn't Ganz's choice to kill the spork joke, but she's part of a process, one that gets guaranteed results, so she must accept the decision and move on.

WHY MOST IDEAS MUST DIE

We've diverged, come up with lots of wild and wonderful ideas – now we need to converge. That means we're going on a killing spree.

While it hurts to 'kill your darlings',[28] you need to face up to the fact that most of your ideas must die. You don't have the time and energy to make them happen and, to be brutally honest, many of them won't be up to much. Sorry about that.

While letting go is never easy, you're going to build a framework for rock-solid decision making, so that you find winners that will be great company as you nurture and grow them.

In this chapter, you're going to choose the best solutions to your problem by:

- Evaluating and critiquing the ideas on offer.

- Working with others to build on ideas.

- Overcoming the paradox of choice to build a personal decision-making framework.

- Getting democratic and asking others to vote on the best.

PERMISSION TO JUDGE IDEAS

One of the rules we set out earlier for running a successful brainstorm is to 'defer judgement of your own and other people's ideas'.

Working with others to generate ideas requires a safe space where all ideas are valued and everyone feels able to contribute. It's important when you're brainstorming that you don't judge – neither self-selecting your own ideas nor criticising other people's. Jenn Maer, IDEO brainstorm supremo explains:

> 'You don't censor yourself during a brainstorm. You're putting every idea out there. Go back through and cull later, but during the brainstorm is not the time to try and decide what's a good idea and what's a bad idea.'

When the time comes to decide – it could be at the end of the brainstorm session or afterwards – you switch to judgement mode. This is when we move from divergent to convergent thinking.

Social psychology researchers have found it to be 'liberating' when people get a chance to debate as part of a brainstorm. Researchers from France and America collaborated on a study which examined the 'tenet' that in brainstorms people are not allowed to criticise their own and others' ideas.[29] Their study compared traditional brainstorming instructions, including the advice not to criticise, with instructions encouraging people to debate and even criticise ideas. They found that:

> 'dissent, debate and competing views have positive value, stimulating divergent and creative thought. Perhaps more importantly, we suggest that the *permission* to criticize

and debate may encourage an atmosphere conducive to idea generation ... Results show the value of both types of instruction, but, in general, debate instructions were superior to traditional brainstorming instructions.'

I'm giving you permission to get critical, but only at the right stage. You first need a safe creative space in which ideas can be generated without criticism. Once you have a multitude of ideas, then you can turn to judgement. You'll hold on to that sense of security as you become more discerning – not all ideas will survive, but having gone through the process of generating numerous options, nothing is wasted. It all contributes to a better solution with a greater chance of success.

BUILDING THE BEST IDEA

Ira Glass described *The Onion*'s editorial meeting as, 'not just tedious, it's the opposite of comedy.' It's also the opposite of most brainstorms, defying rules of creative collaboration by going around the table reading out solo ideas, often to jeers from fellow writers.

But what *The Onion* excels at is building on ideas through the process of debate. Glass said the staff were nice to each other – they were just tough on the material. It's not personal criticism but professional – a slight but important difference that centres on the creative output, not the creator.

The comedy writers minutely dissect all the jokes, and over the years, he explains: 'they've developed a way of discussing the material to decide whether something is so outstandingly funny it beats a lot of other jokes that are also pretty funny, and what makes each joke funny, and how to make it funnier.'

The writers' job is to choose which of the 600 headlines pitched that week make it into the final sixteen. To decide, they have developed a system for figuring out the outstandingly funny from the pretty funny. Can you work out why 'Local girlfriend always wants to do stuff' made the cut, while the near identical 'Nation's girlfriends call for more quality time' got jeered off the table?

Their process, a so-called, 'hive mentality', uses criteria and a shared language to categorise headlines as silly, too silly, silly in the wrong way, or meeting the ultimate goal of being a 'laffer' – the big-hitting, dumb jokes that are the most popular and most shared jokes from the website.

If *The Onion*'s Monday meeting is all about choosing potential headlines, then Tuesday is about evaluating and exploring the shortlist.

In the last chapter, Jenn Maer talked of the collaborative approach at IDEO, where she described how people working together build on each other's ideas so that 'you can't ever tell where an idea came from by the time you get it out the door.' Comedy is famously competitive and cut-throat, but by the time the writers meet on Tuesday, their job is to work together to improve the jokes.

Once a headline has made it onto the table, it becomes shared property – the idea maker has to let go and the joke is no longer their personal responsibility. The writers re-pitch the shortlisted headlines, and together they dissect them, asking, 'What will we say about that? Where does that joke go?'

The approach overcomes the so-called 'founder bias', which happens when someone becomes overly attached to their idea and their favouritism prevents rational thinking. Remember Megan Ganz's heartbreak when her joke was rejected? It's only natural for us to feel the attachment of founder bias, but in holding on, we're succumbing to cognitive biases that prevent us from having the best ideas. So, forget about individual wins, and focus instead on gains for your audience.

Back at *The Onion*, they collaborate to build on jokes, going wild and silly, to push them harder and make them as funny as possible. This shared ownership is extended to the next round where another team of writers creates the stories that build on headlines and finds pictures to hammer home the punchline.

While collaboration is important, what maximises your chance of picking a winner is team diversity. Professor Paul Nutt, who researches business decisions, found that the chances of making good choices are improved when you work in a group with multiple perspectives. Diversity is essential to good ideas.[30]

THE PARADOX OF CHOICE

While it's great to have multiple ideas, we can get overwhelmed deciding between them. Research shows that when the pressure is on to decide, we become less likely to make a decision when there are more options available. Welcome to the paradox of choice.

A series of studies overturned the assumption that more choices lead to better decisions. It has been shown that in the face of abundant options – such as the many brilliant ideas you've come up with – people become burdened by the responsibility of distinguishing between good and bad choices. And it's not just big life decisions that overwhelm us; we sweat the small stuff just as much. Take a simple purchasing decision such as choosing a jar of jam.

Researchers from New York and California set up a stall selling 24 varieties of jam at a posh farmers' market.[31] On another day, they laid out only six types of jam. While the larger display gained much more interest, the people who browsed were one tenth as likely to buy jam as the people who saw the smaller display. It seems that people enjoy having an abundance of choices, but when it comes to acting on them, they become paralysed and unable to choose, even when the choice is over something as trivial as jam.

This study has been replicated with all sorts of other decisions, including big life decisions like picking financial services, and the paradox of choice has become a central plank in behavioural sciences.

As a general principle, fewer choices are more likely to lead to action, and that's exactly what we want with your idea – to make it happen. Let's dive in and make some decisions.

MAKING DECISIONS BY YOURSELF

The first step in making good decisions is to define criteria. In the same way that *The Onion* categorised jokes from silly all the way up to a 'laffer', you too need some way of defining what success looks like for a hustle idea.

For companies working on new product ideas, the criteria might be whether it will make a certain amount of money, whether they have staff with the skills to deliver it, or whether it is within their market. For individual hustlers, you might look at whether it's cheap to do, how easy it is, whether it excites and motivates you, whether it's something that would make your mother proud or your friends jealous, or whether it will give you the lifestyle you desire or attract million-dollar investments.

When making a criteria-based decision, you need to commit to that approach rather than overthrow the decision and trust your gut – so says Nobel Prize-winning behavioural economist Daniel Kahneman. In his book *Thinking, Fast and Slow*, he outlines the two decision-making systems of the brain. System 1 is automatic and fast while System 2 is deliberate and slow. The conflict between these two systems is why many decisions seem so hard. For example, your gut feeling tells you something isn't quite right, even when everyone says it is right.

In the book, Kahneman suggests an approach for evaluating candidates in job interviews; let's apply this same approach to interview your idea. You have mind mapped or brainstormed a whole bunch of potential solutions – these are your idea candidates. Before considering them:

- Write a list of no more than six criteria.

- Draw up a grid listing the ideas against the criteria.

- Decide on a scoring system, such as giving marks out of five.

- Go through each idea and score them against the list.

- Tally up the scores and you'll have a winner.

When you get the results, commit to choosing the idea with the highest score – even if your gut says no. While it might feel wrong, research has shown that this is by far the most effective way to pick the best idea.

ENLISTING OTHERS TO HELP YOU CHOOSE

While you're perfectly capable of applying criteria and choosing an idea by yourself, it can sometimes help to get other people involved with the decision. This is especially true if you've already fallen in love with all of your ideas and choosing one feels like asking a parent to choose which of their children they would save from a burning building.

Enlist some friends or co-workers to choose between your idea candidates. This can also be a great way to wrap up a brainstorm – you've already asked people to get involved and they'll be keen to see what happens next.

The first step is communicating the ideas. You need to make sure they are presented in the same way, so that they don't favour the best turned-out idea. The next chapter will give you some ways to name, draw, write and present ideas – but for now, settle on a simple format, such as a one sentence summary written on a Post-it note and stuck on a wall.

Give everyone the same number of votes. This will stop the idea-creator or the most senior person getting more sway.[32] When I run brainstorms, I hand out three votes to everyone and they choose whether to allocate all three to one idea or spread them across three ideas.

After everyone has voted, tally up the results and go with the first past the post.[33]

A FINAL SENSE CHECK

If you're feeling paralysed by choice, trust the data and go with either your own assessment or what democracy decides. While that's easy for me to say, you might be plagued by doubts. If so, here's a final sense check from innovation expert and startup founder Sam Reid of ThinkSprint.

Reid suggests you interrogate your decision, checking your idea against the following criteria. Is it:

- Technically feasible?

- Practically feasible?

- Financially feasible?

Finally, ask yourself the critical question: 'Would I really care about this idea if I were the target audience?'

Channel your personas and empathise with their needs and wants. What you're looking for is a booming 'hell yes' to give you that motivational push to keep going as you build, test and hustle your idea into the world.

Now that you've chosen an idea, you need to hone it. In the next chapter, you'll find out how to name, write, draw and prototype – the first stage of getting it into the world. Before we move on to creation, let's pull together a rough plan of action.

A ROUGH PLAN

Planning is tough. Even sense-checking Sam Reid struggled with it, admitting he was terrible at planning: 'I just ploughed forwards, usually into a rut.' By reading up on the benefits and process of planning, he stopped falling into ruts with his ideas.

The benefit, he says, of having a plan before you embark is that it:

> 'creates a set of mental stepping stones into the distance. They will never be perfect; however, just knowing you can put one foot in front of the other to make progress reduces a lot of anxiety and makes you go faster in the long run. With ThinkSprint, we spent two years plotting the stepping stones before we set off properly on them, but we now know exactly where we are going and how to get there.'

Reid has a simple template with a step-by-step timeline for an idea and what happens at each stage. He uses it with ThinkSprint founders and project managers to force them to work through all the critical elements.

It might feel too early to do this – as you're not really sure what's coming next – but throw down a few notes on what you're going to do. Namely, what the stages are, the main deliverables for each of those steps, and who can help you achieve them. Write it as a simple list or grid with the timeline across the top.

The benefits of having even a rough plan have been proven time and again. Planning helps you translate an intention, the desire or dream of doing something, into action. Having an implementation plan that specifies what, when and how you will do something has been shown to increase the chances you'll do it, and do it faster.[34]

FROM KILLING TO CREATION

Choosing ideas is hard, even for battle-hardened comedians. Take this headline that made it into the Tough Room at *The Onion*: 'Ghost just dropped by to say boo.' To say it divided the writers is an understatement – one writer walked out in protest and the fight over whether it was funny got so serious that the editor-in-chief had to intervene. That joke survived, but nearly a million jokes have died at that table.[35]

It's not easy killing off ideas, but it's necessary – you don't have the time to make them all happen. Don't take it personally and don't get too attached; trust the process and keep moving forwards.

This chapter provided you with some approaches to making choices that prevent the crippling overwhelm you might feel when faced with lots of potentially great ideas. Enlisting the support of other people makes culling ideas easier and more fun.

CHAPTER SUMMARY

- **In short**: Stop fretting about choosing and get ready to kill ideas so you can take the best one forward.

- **Start now**: Write a list of decision-making criteria to help you choose.

- **Go expert**: Trust democracy and enlist others to take the pressure off deciding.

- **Be happy**: Check if your idea has the 'hell yes' factor, that will motivate you to keep going.

- **Next step**: Grab your winning idea – it's time to make it real.

2 Honing ideas

5 PROTOTYPE

name it   draw   build

6 COMMUNICATE

pitch   tell a story   gather feedback

7 TEST

MVP   experiment   gather evidence

8 VALIDATE

Data   Sell sell sell   plan   money

CHAPTER FIVE

Prototype

It was go-time for Anne-Marie Imafidon. The 23 year old had an idea to inspire girls to study STEM subjects (science, technology, engineering and maths). She needed to make an intervention early in a girl's life because choices made at school can lock women out of careers later.

She'd done her research and knew there was a big problem: not only were women under-represented in technology jobs, but the numbers were going backwards. She was determined to act. Then – bang – she landed some funding from Telefonica/O2's Go Think Big programme.

She called her idea the Stemettes Project, but to have the impact she dreamt of, the project needed to be more than a name.

'Every good idea starts with a domain,' Imafidon says. 'I set up a Twitter account and Facebook page, I set up a Gmail with the logo, and started writing and tweeting about it.' Her idea had a presence in the world, and people could interact with it. This was February 2013. Soon, she was beginning conversations about the problem, and people were reaching out to her. Including the British prime minister. Ten months after setting up her domain, Imafidon went for a meeting at Number 10 Downing Street. Imafidon calls it 'literally magic'.

Amazing things happen when you get ideas out of your head and into the world. You just need to take the first steps to make it real, like: give it a name, buy a domain, tell someone about it, show them something.

STOP DREAMING, START DOING

Paul-Jervis Heath describes his work at design agency Modern Human as 'reducing the distance between idea and actual product launch'. He believes you need to quickly prove they work. 'Until your product gets to market,' Heath says, 'it's all hypothetical.'

Ideas can change the world and fulfil your every ambition, but to have real impact, they need to be real. That's where prototyping comes in.

A prototype helps you prove your idea. It involves making something – and it's not just about code, tech or construction – you can prototype a product, a service or an experience.

'Start prototyping as soon as you're developing your ideas,' Heath says. 'You want to work out what's the simplest possible version of that product that you could release, and get it out to test it in the marketplace.'

You need to forget about perfection, stop spending time developing a full product, and instead move fast to create something tangible.

YOU HAVE EVERYTHING YOU NEED

In the last chapter, you chose something work on; now you need to make it happen. This is a scary moment. You stop dabbling in the make-believe and start making. This is the point where many people give up, the fear gets to them, the excuses start. In fact, this is where the fun begins.

Channel your messy childhood self, the one who made mud pies, and built dens and sandcastle towers. At the end of the day, you'd clean off the muck, pack up your grand design, or wait for the sea to wash away your masterpiece. The adventure would begin anew the next day. There's nothing like getting your hands dirty, rolling up your sleeves and getting stuck in.

But, but ... I hear your excuses: *I can't build anything. I can't code a website. I can't do it. I don't have the skills, the time, the experience, the money.*

You have everything you need.

You just need to start. Start small. Start by asking: what's the quickest, cheapest and smallest version I can share? The answer is often a name, a one-sentence description or a sketch.

Imafidon advises not overthinking it. 'You have this idea,' she says, 'and the cool thing is you never really know where it will go. Let's just do it and see what happens.'

It's go-time. We're going to get that idea of yours into the world. The magic is about to happen. Over the coming chapter, you'll get hands-on, and:

- Give your idea a snappy name.

- Summarise it in a sentence.

- Write it, draw it, make a prototype to share your idea.

- Let go of perfection and focus on fun.

NAME YOUR IDEA

Words are power. They will transform your vague, woolly idea into a named entity. Writing takes something from your imagination and makes a mark on the world, in ink.

Naming your idea is the first stage of honing it: giving it clarity, helping you improve it and building momentum as you make it happen.

So, what will you call it?

A good name sticks and will make your idea memorable. But names are hard, so it might take some playing around to figure one out. Here are a few tips to guide you:

- Keep it short and punchy, as well as easy to pronounce and spell. It should resonate with your audience, but avoid jargon.

- A really good name goes beyond the practical and connects emotionally. For example, imagine how your audience will feel when they achieve success thanks to using your product.

- Finally, it should be unique. A quick online search can confirm this. At this early stage, don't spend too much time checking out competitors and finding a domain; just focus on the name's ability to communicate your concept, and what it does for people.

It will eventually become a brand, with a logo, website and perhaps a trademark, but for now just naming it will make it feel concrete, real and exciting.

Enjoy the process of coming up with a name, create a mind map or have a brainstorm, build and create new versions – go wild. If it feels too complicated, add some constraints. A startup consultant I know plays Countdown with her founders, forcing them to create names from a limited selection of letters – a classic innovation technique for stimulating creative thinking.

Nicole Raby, the student working on her final-year project, brainstormed names for her campus event-location app. She considered: CampusExplore, Mapexplore, CampusConnect, Campus Life, Discover-Campus, Campus map and CampusTrack. She plumped for DiscoverCampus.

Do I follow my own advice? Prolifiko, the startup I co-founded, sounds amazing when you say it, especially if you go all Italian and elongate the vowel sounds so it rolls off the tongue. However, people really struggle to read it or spell it. On the plus side, we got the dotcom, but if you can't spell it ... Like I said, names are hard.

WRITE YOUR CONCEPT

In innovation, when you write down an idea, it becomes a concept. There's a simple framework for structuring a concept, consisting of four elements that give your idea a bit more polish and shine. These are:

1. Name

2. Problem

3. Solution

4. Benefit

Let's break it down, starting with the bits you've covered in previous exercises.

Name

You've nailed that. Next.

What problem are you looking at?

You've got this one covered, because it's how you developed your idea. Think about your user, the people with the problem and their pains and gains.

What solution are you offering?

This part explains in super simple terms how your solution works. Think about how it solves the problem, what it does, and how this meets someone's needs.

What benefits do people gain from using it?

This takes a bit more explanation. The mistake some people make when explaining their idea is they focus on features, rather than benefits – there is a world of difference between the two.

To illustrate this, imagine a chair. What are the features of a chair? It has four legs, a seat and a back – these are common to all chairs, and it's hard to differentiate between this chair with four legs and that one with four legs. The benefits are what will distinguish and sell this chair. For example, the reclining position means that this chair will allow you to put your feet up after a long day at work; that chair is made of wipe-clean plastic, which is perfect for messy children at dinner time. By communicating benefits, you sell a solution to people's problems.

Keep the audience in mind: think about what they will get from your product, how it will it make their day – or their life – better. It's all about tangible benefits, so be specific.

Do it now: express your idea in a few sentences following this four-step structure. Keep your concept statement short and simple. Don't judge. Don't be perfectionist.

This is your first attempt at defining your idea, and as a first draft it will go through many tweaks and changes as you iterate and improve. Done is better than perfect, so just get it down.

If you thrive under constraints, write your concept in a tweet. Start with Twitter's current, positively verbose, 280-character limit, then sharpen it down to the original 140-character limit, and finally, do it in 60 characters – that's the limit set by tech launch website Product Hunt.

Let's see how Nicole Raby described Discover-Campus. Her first one-sentence version was:

> *DiscoverCampus is an app that uses GPS-location, displaying an interactive map of your university campus that pinpoints the location of all types of different events added by anyone, outlets for food and drink, while also exploring offers and discounts around campus for students.*

It's a clear outline of what the app is and does and the features it includes. It's missing, however, the benefit to students, especially freshers who are feeling overwhelmed and unsure where to start. How about this for a revised version, still under 280 characters but with the benefits added in:

> *DiscoverCampus helps students to quickly and cheaply find entertainment, food and drink that they love on their university campus. The*

app uses GPS location-tracking technology to send tailored information about events, outlets and special offers near them that are happening now.

In 140 characters:

Want to find the best events, music, food, drink and discounts near you now? Do more, save money. Find your scene fast and never miss out again.

In 60 characters:

Find the best events, get there quick, meet friends, use discounts.

PROTOTYPING: LET'S GET PHYSICAL

A prototype is the first version of your idea, a physical manifestation of what was once theoretical. Its purpose is to get across your concept, without having to build a full working model. Think of it as a prop that helps you tell the story of your idea to stimulate interest, discussion and feedback.

It's not the final product and won't work properly. It can, and should, be pretty messy. This isn't about perfection or testing how it works – it's about gauging the market and getting initial feedback on the concept.

Making a prototype is fun – both the process and the outcome. When I worked in innovation, there was genuine delight when I'd open my box of coloured pens, crayons, paper, egg boxes, scissors, glue, as well as Lego bricks, a couple of dolls and anything else I'd found in the toy section of the charity shop. Many design agencies have prototyping rooms or sheds in their offices – alongside toys they often include serious tech, like 3D printers and precision cutters for metal and plastic. Many large towns and cities have what are called makers' labs, where you can go along for training and book sessions to work with others to build physical prototypes.

There are lots of options available, so whether you're working by yourself at home – breaking out the cardboard and double-sided sticky tape, or using online tools and tutorials – or have access to a makers' lab with professional training, prototyping is possible for everyone.

At the end of a prototyping session, you get something tangible to see, hold and interact with. You'll feel very proud of your ugly creation, but don't fall in love! Think of your prototype as just a fling on the way to a relationship with your final product or service. You're using it share and gather feedback, and you can build a new one tomorrow if you want to upgrade it or gather fresh feedback.

MANY WAYS TO BUILD

Some of you might be feeling a bit sceptical at this point and tempted to skip the next section – you've been adulting for a while now, and you do not want your attempts to be taken seriously undone by whipping out a tinfoil robot at your next meeting.

You don't need to cover things in glitter and sparkles to get a response from your audience; you can build stuff without having to get your hands dirty. Let's look at some of the many ways to build a prototype.

Write it

Writing is a simple and cheap way to communicate your idea. Words can 'build' a prototype. If you like to see things in full sentences, then grab a pen. You can write a blog, a story or a script to pitch your idea – Amazon gets its product managers to write a press release for their new products before they have made anything.

You can prototype writing too; the prototype of this book was a proposal that was read by agents and publishers. Rather than spending months writing the whole thing, you can write back cover copy for a book, an advert for a movie or the trailer for a TV sitcom and share with people to see what they think.

Draw it

Drawing an idea might mean the initial sketches you use as directions to build something physical, or the drawing might be the actual prototype that you share. This is called paper prototyping, where you map out the experience for the person using it. It works equally well for services as for digital products. For example, if your idea is for a shop or theme park, you can sketch out each stage of someone's visit. If you are creating an app or website, you draw the screens and buttons that people would use.

There's more advice to come on drawing and using online tools, so read on if you need a skills (or confidence) boost.

Make it

Classic prototyping is building something physical. You can get creative at home, join a makers' day or visit a makers' lab where they'll have all the kit you need.

Present it

Use presentation software like PowerPoint or Keynote to mock up designs, such a screens for a website or app. You can use your designs in a pretend product video to fake how people would move through the website. Add some graphics, a voiceover and music and – ta-da! – you've got an all-singing, all-dancing product to wow your audience.

Code it

If you've got an idea for software, you could create an online version, but don't build the full thing. Think interactive mock-ups that link screens together rather than a fully functional website or app. Much like a paper prototype, this type of mock-up shows sample screens that users scroll, swipe or click through to mimic the experience of using a digital product. You can check online for the latest tools – there are new ones released every day. Search for the best prototyping tools for beginners, and if you fancy going pro, search for mock-up tools for user interface or user experience design.

Fake it

Can't code? Then worry not; just create a fake website. If making a landing page feels overwhelming, how about creating a Google or Facebook ad that people click on, or using a survey to gather feedback? Experiment with different virtual versions for people to interact with.

Concierge it

Like its hotel-dwelling namesake, there's no tech involved in a concierge prototype – just you running around making bookings and reservations, and buying and delivering products and services. The archetypal concierge service was Zappos, which created an online store for shoes: when they received an order, they would run out to a shop, buy the shoes and post them. Strictly speaking it's more than a prototype, but it shows that all types of ideas can be created at this early stage.

Having read the options above, you might have landed on the perfect prototype. Hold your horses! Having more than one idea leads to better ideas as you say 'and, yes' to build on the first thing you thought of. Take a few minutes to generate some prototyping options.

BRAINSTORM A PROTOTYPE

You're going to flex your creative thinking muscles again as we put your brainstorming skills to work. You'll generate different options for how to prototype your winning solution and then narrow down to one that you can achieve. Remember you're not building the full thing, just enough to capture the concept and make something tangible that you can share with people for feedback.

Start by asking: How might I make the smallest, simplest version that I can show to people?

By now you know exactly who your idea is for, so have them at the front of your mind. Imagine showing them your prototype; think about what might interest and excite them, and what they would like to look at, hold or play with.

Start generating options. You can work alone, perhaps by creating a mind map where each option branches off and triggers new possibilities, or in a group where you generate ideas together using Post-it notes. Check out Chapter 3 if you need a reminder.

Once you've generated possibilities, choose the one that best fits your criteria – this will include being cheap and speedy to make, and in line with your skills, access to tools, and what feels fun to do.

EIGHT IS THE MAGIC NUMBER

Another exercise to get the ideas flowing comes from Google Ventures, called Crazy 8s – not because the ideas are crazy, but because of its fast-paced approach to generating ideas.[36] It can be done by yourself, as a warm up to a group brainstorm, or as a complete session. Start with the problem statement, or 'How might we ...?' question.

Grab a piece of A4 paper and fold it into eight equal-sized sections. Do this by folding it in half, then in half again, and again – the three folds will give you eight panels.

Your task is to draw something in each panel. Use a combination of words and sketches to thrash out the idea.

Set a timer for eight minutes and go!

As with all timed exercises, the frantic pace reduces the time for overthinking and judging your work. Just get stuff down, quickly and messily. I find the first couple of sketches take the longest, then you speed up as the time races away from you. Often the later ideas improve on earlier ones, taking one element and iterating it.

When the timer goes off, review your sketches. You might find there are a couple of ideas you would like to build on; if so, set the timer and go again. Or perhaps take one idea and draw it on a bigger sheet of paper.

See the illustration below, which draws out the process of how might we choose a plant online. Each frame moves us towards finding our dream cactus.

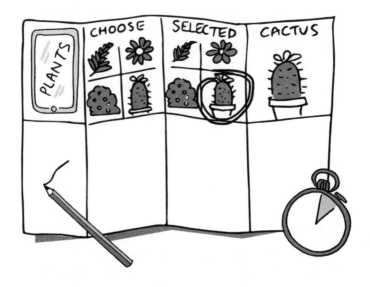

PROTOTYPE IN UNDER AN HOUR

When people are asked what the biggest barriers are to making ideas happen, they say having no time and no money. I believe these 'barriers' can be your biggest assets – reframe these constraints and use them to foster creativity.

In my innovation workshops, I take a group of people from having no ideas at all to rapid prototyping in under an hour – using limited time and resources. I'm ruthless with time keeping and only let people use the pens and paper I've got with me. It has worked with hundreds of people, over and over again.

Find an hour in your week, set the clock, get ready, go!

Brainstorm

Return to the concept you worked up at the end of Chapter 4. Start to imagine it in the world: what it might look and feel like, and what features it might have. If you were explaining it to someone, what would you want to show them?

Draw a mind map or make some simple sketches – the Crazy 8 exercise is perfect to get ideas flowing.

Choose

Look over your brainstorm and pick the top ideas.

Sketch it

Before you start to build, sketch out a single concept, one that includes the important features – or moments if you're designing an experience or service.

Remember, you're not putting everything into a single concept – it's a simple blueprint from idea to prototype.

Build it

Grab whatever pens, paint, paper and crafts supplies you have, and use the rest of the hour to build a rough prototype. It's not meant to be perfect, so stop worrying and start having some fun. Make something – get creative and play with what's possible.

Your prototype is a prop that will bring your idea to life. In the next chapter, you'll use it to tell the story of your idea and gather feedback.

EXTREME PROTOTYPING: THE HACKATHON

If you want to get serious about building stuff, you can try a hackathon. In essence, it's a collaborative problem-solving event; someone provides the venue, food, a problem to solve and everything you need to make it happen against the clock – often in 24 or 48 hours.

Hackathons have a whiff of unwashed coders locked in a battle to build, without bathroom breaks. But many organisations are changing the narrative, like Anne-Marie Imafidon, whose startup Stemettes was designed in response to the macho image of hackathons. She explains: 'If you're a girl under eighteen, there was no space for you to go to because they have beer on tap and it's 48 hours and during the night.' They were not safe spaces for teenage girls.

Rather than avoid them, she suggests you learn from what's happening and design a simpler version:

> 'You don't want to over bake it. If there's a particular problem you're coming together to solve, it might be that you assemble a group of friends. You say, "Well this is what it is. We've done some reading and seen this person's solved it that way. That person's solved it that way." Then together you figure out how you want to do it.'

Take inspiration from other hackathons to design your own version. I did this for a side hustle several of us were working on while we had full-time jobs. We met at my house one Saturday and set a goal for the day – taking a full day to work together moved us forward in leaps and bounds, compared to squeezing in an hour or so at the end of our working days.

My advice is to agree tasks, responsibilities and who is working with whom; give people the freedom to do it their way but come together to update on progress at regular intervals; and be realistic about what you can achieve in limited time. And don't forget to agree who's buying the drinks for the end of hackathon celebrations.

MASTERCLASS: DRAW YOUR CONCEPT

'Words are really dangerous,' says Paul-Jervis Heath, 'because the same word can mean an awful lot of things to an awful lot of people.'

His solution to the slipperiness of language is to draw something. 'When we describe a concept,' Heath says, 'people come up with a picture of what they think that means.' But when we draw a concept, it encourages us to be specific and precise about what we mean, so that people have the same image and understanding of the concept as we do.

Drawing is an important part of the design process at his agency Modern Human. Heath always starts on paper rather than on a computer package, because people don't get too attached to paper. 'If you've spent twenty minutes drawing something on paper,' he says, 'you can photocopy it, change it, and start again, or throw it away. You get much less attached to ideas by keeping it on paper.' Drawing requires no specialist skills. 'It's a great leveller,' says Heath. 'We can all draw.'

Graphic facilitator Cara Holland couldn't agree more. 'Working visually is a super power,' she says, 'that ability to really connect with people in a way that other forms of communication miss out.'

Holland has worked with some of the biggest brands in the world, from Sony, Google, Microsoft, Time Warner, to the BBC and the NHS. She sees visual working not as art, but as communication:

> 'Everything we do in the business world is trying to connect with people. Whether you're selling somebody something, spreading the word about your product, helping people do something, or explaining what your passion project is about. Whatever the purpose behind it, it's all about trying to connect, to communicate well and get people engaged. There is no better way of doing that, than visually.'

At this stage, you are creating a prototype to show people. It's not the full working product, just a first version. Having a sketch of your idea, or a paper prototype that walks people through how it works, is a great way to get people to interact and give feedback that will help you hone your concept. Holland says:

> 'Get stuff out of your head onto a page where everybody can see the same information at the same time. It cuts through all the rubbish, cuts through all the waffle. If you add visuals, you bring the clarity that people need to engage with it fully and understand it properly, and therefore comment on it or develop it more effectively. Visuals help every step of the way.'

Working visually isn't hard, but it involves overcoming psychological barriers, the narrative many of us have that we can't draw, that we're not artistic, that we'll make a fool of ourselves.

Holland believes everyone can communicate visually. In the work she does with her visual thinking studio Graphic Change and in her book *Draw a Better Business*, she builds people's skills and confidence so they can share their ideas with the world, win jobs and give pitches and presentations.[37] Here are her top tips to get started.

HOW TO DRAW

Don't be scared.

Stop being super self-critical and self-conscious; be kind to yourself. Find small ways to begin. Get the basics under your belt. Start super simple and enjoy the mistakes.

Draw less.

It's not art – it's all about functional drawing. Keep that in mind and embrace working simply.

Don't be too artistic.

The time you spend adding fancy stuff and making it beautiful and complicated is time you could have used to communicate more content.

Be bold.

Sketchy pencil lines will be lost on the audience for your drawing. So, work big and work bold. Use a big marker pen with the broadest nib you can find and a flip chart or large sheets of paper to give impact.

Don't be clever.

No visual puns! None of that works because it excludes people who don't get your joke or don't have your grasp of the English language.

Limit your colour.

Start with a black felt tip as it's easy to see. Pick one contrasting colour if you need to highlight key elements.

Draw something every day.

There are no magical shortcuts; you just need to practise. The more you do it, the less afraid of it you'll be.

Finally, show people.

Getting comfortable with being seen is really important. Find an ally to share your drawings with who you know will be kind; the aim at the start is not to ask for feedback but just to show somebody what you're doing. Then show people stuff regularly so that sharing a prototype is not some big ta-da moment that you stand or fall on.

Draw it now: grab some paper and pens, and do a few sketches of your concept. You might draw your product or service, or someone using it, or how they feel afterwards – or you might draw your product logo or name in colours.

DREAM IT, BUILD IT, SHARE IT

Rather than focussing on your drawing or technical skills, focus instead on the purpose of communicating your concept.

'I can't think of another communication tool,' says visual thinker Holland, 'that brings you that clarity that drawing does. It helps you have conversations that are more collaborative and more equal because everybody can see and understand the same information. It's super clear.'

Working with your hands to draw or build something helps you at every stage of the process – to make something new, figure things out, hone your idea, explain it, and get people excited about it.

Holland tells me: 'If you can't draw it, you can't do it. When you're either developing, refining or reviewing something, if it can't be drawn then you've got real problems.'

Fundamentally, that's why prototyping is such an important test of your idea: if you can't explain it, write it or draw it, you'll struggle to build it and win people over to your vision.

It is a skill that requires practice, but one that's worth the effort, as it allows you to effectively get across your ideas in a short space of time. And if you need persuading further, drawing and prototyping reduces stress and strengthens neural pathways – just what you need as you build your happy hustle.

ANY WAY YOU CAN, JUST DO IT

'Expressing ideas,' says Jennifer Aldrich, 'is not directly related to how beautifully they're relayed. I think people respond to the cartoons because they relate to them – they don't need to be pixel-perfect masterpieces to make people feel something. That was a big lesson for me, since I've always considered myself artistically challenged.'

Aldrich is famous for drawing stick figures on her blog User Experience Rocks; she's also senior manager of design community partnership at InVisionApp, the prototyping software.[38] Aldrich is a cheerleader for making ideas happen, as she says: 'Just get your ideas out of your head in any way you can, and go from there.'

Don't make excuses for your drawing ability – just use whatever skills you have and whatever tools you can get your hands on, and do it.

Aldrich laughs at her own inability to draw, yet she knows the life-changing power of a doodle – a very sketchy drawing on her blog went viral and brought her a huge amount of positive attention. All she was trying to do was explain something to her daughter by drawing a bicycle. Her daughter got the message, and so did tens of thousands of other people.

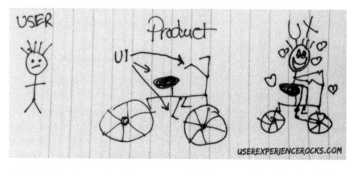

© Jennifer Aldrich, reprinted with permission

She also gives this example of the power of a sketch, from her first startup: 'Our VP drew a doodle on a napkin during lunch one day, and it turned into what became our flagship product that was acquired years later for nine figures.'

In her work for InVision, Aldrich champions digital design, without the need for any specialist skills or training. 'Rapid prototyping,' she explains, 'allows you to create some mock-ups, hot spot them together in seconds, and immediately test your idea with your target audience. Being able to identify whether or not your idea should proceed, be adjusted or be tossed out that early in the process is incredibly powerful and a no-brainer from a financial perspective.'

This is exactly what cash-strapped student Nicole Raby did when she needed to create a prototype for her project. With no drawing or design skills, she hit Google to find some tools, then downloaded a well-reviewed, entry-level prototyping product that required no experience. After watching some YouTube explainer videos, she started creating.

'I started making a logo for my app, then some basic graphics, then some pages,' Raby says. 'I've made a login page to make it feel realistic. It was complicated at first because I didn't know how to use it. Even now it's difficult, but it's fun, because it's different to what I normally do.'

With a bit of research and some practice, Raby soon had a prototype that brought her idea to life, one she could show people and use to gather feedback. We're going to find out how to communicate your idea in the next chapter, but before we do that, a note on perfectionism. Drawing, building and making prototypes can be frustrating, as you get to grips with your lack of skills, and it can be embarrassing when the physical version of your idea fails to meet your perfect mental image. But that's what makes the process so fulfilling – learning something new, having fun, and getting better the more you do it.

Take Jennifer Aldrich, who says: 'I built my first website in the 90s and had a blast doing it. It was a giant hot mess covered in animated gifs – I cringe every time I think about it, but I loved every second of creating it.'

So, let go of perfection. Focus on fun and fulfilment. Any way you can do it – just do it.

CHAPTER SUMMARY

- **In short**: Get your idea out of your head and into the world with a prototype.

- **Start now**: Brainstorm ways you can create a version of your concept, or try the Crazy 8s to get ideas flowing.

- **Go expert**: Buy in some kit or go to a makers' space to build a physical prototype.

- **Be happy**: Making stuff is fun and fulfilling as you learn from your mistakes and build new skills.

- **Next step**: Share your concept with people.

CHAPTER SIX

Communicate

George Bettany spent four years trying to build a startup with his co-founder James Routledge. It was hard work and took a toll on them – physically and mentally. Routledge began having anxiety attacks, which he wrote about on his blog. A simple blog post, just 500 words long, changed everything for the two friends.

Within a week, the blog had 20,000 hits, and they received nearly 600 emails. Bettany explains: 'It got an amazing response. We had thousands of people saying, "I feel the same way. I get it. Thank you so much for talking about it."'

THE UNINTENTIONAL PROTOTYPE

'It was so clear to us because we'd never felt that kind of response before,' Bettany says. 'So, we knew we had to pursue it. We didn't know it was a prototype, we didn't know it was a business, we didn't know it was a product or anything. We just knew that people really valued it.'

Bettany and Routledge went on to create Sanctus, a startup changing the perception of mental health. It now employs over twenty coaches – trained mental health professionals – who facilitate difficult conversations about mental health in the workplace, working with over 500 individuals a month.

'We both started to talk about our feelings, basically, for the first time,' Bettany says. 'I just don't think people expected it from me or James.'

By making their conversation public, they had prototyped an idea. They took a problem they were both grappling with and started to figure out a solution, getting feedback from people who felt the same. They started with a blog and iterated until they landed on the best format for Sanctus – we'll hear more about that process later.

Jenn Maer from IDEO considers prototyping to be the most important process in making ideas happen. She says: 'Just be willing to try things in really small, low fidelity ways – what's the smallest move that I can make to find out if something's going to work – and then keep prototyping it until something really sticks and catches fire.'

Making stuff matters. Sharing it gives you the feedback to make it better. One of Maer's IDEO colleagues, Dennis Boyle, has a rule never to attend a meeting without a prototype. Having a prototype, even just a link to a blog post, or a screenshot on your mobile, will communicate your concept and generate reactions from people.

Bettany describes the response to the blog being like a 'pull'. He and Routledge had spent years on their first startup 'pushing' their idea into the market with little or no reaction; then they found themselves in a situation where they were being pulled by the demand to do something. He says: 'We had more love in a 500-word piece online than we had in years of building a whole product and raising lots of money.'

Whether you plan your prototype meticulously or it happens by accident, sharing it with people can change everything. Bettany and Routledge wrote their prototype; you might have drawn yours, built it, or mocked it up online. Whatever you've made, you're going to take your prototype into the world and introduce it to a few friendly faces. Over the coming chapter, you'll build the confidence to:

- Write an elevator pitch.

- Share your story with people.

- Gather initial feedback.

- Evaluate the responses you receive.

GIVE YOUR IDEA IMPACT

'Even if it's in a small way, and you worry it won't work out, think about creative ways to solve a problem you think is worth looking at,' says Anjali Ramachandran. 'You never know where it will lead you, and what it can do for the world.'

Ramachandran is an inspiration. One of the co-founders of Ada's List, the global community for women working in technology, she started Other Valleys, a newsletter that champions world-changing ideas from emerging markets to counter the narrative of US/UK dominance. Both projects were side hustles to her job at the time working in innovation for a global communications and media buying agency. In the day job, Ramachandran regularly invited startup founders to present to the business, to help stimulate new ways of thinking and forge partnerships.

She says: 'It's the smaller entrepreneurs and businesses that often make a big impact, because they're solving problems the bigger companies find too small for their commercial liking. And over time, that impact grows.'

While startups might have the edge over corporates for speed, Ramachandran found that startups could also learn a thing or two from large commercial organisations. These are her takeaways:

> 'Be clear about your business idea and plan. I can't tell you the number of startups I met who were not able to give me a clear two-minute elevator pitch, or who were not able to articulate their USP compared to competitors. And yes, every business has a competitor, even if it is a Facebook group. By saying "no one" is a competitor, it shows you up as someone who hasn't bothered to do basic market research!'

Ramachandran recommends that startups, even very early prototype-stage ones, look ahead to the future and learn to pitch their big vision. In the early stages, investors need to see a clearly articulated vision to believe in an idea. Later in the book, we'll look at how you can pull together a basic business plan, accounting for market size, opportunity and competition. But for now, she recommends asking yourself:

'What do you want to be known for ten or twenty years from now? And then work backwards to find out what you have to do now to get there. Good strategy is very much long-term, or at least starts from long-term thinking as opposed to short-term tactics. Many people are so focussed on doing their job well *now* that they fail to realise that working with a longer-term goal in mind helps them do their job better in the now.'

She's right – looking ahead to the future and imagining success is also proven to engage neural pathways, making connections in the brain as if you *have already* achieved your goal. That triggers the release of feel-good brain chemical dopamine and gives you just the boost you need to take action.

You've got a prototype, now it's time to share it. Take encouragement from Ramachandran:

'Solving problems may not be everyone's cup of tea, but if people who feel strongly about contributing to a world they want to live in and leaving a legacy for the next generation do even a small bit, it *will* make a difference to an audience that feels the same way as you do – and that audience exists, however big or small.'

You can do it. Let's wow Ramachandran with your difference-making, world-changing, prototype.

SHARE YOUR CONCEPT

Imagine you overhear your boss pitching your idea. Your blood boils. *You* came up with it, and she's taking all the damn credit. But, when asked to explain how she came up with the idea, she stumbles. She wants the glory but has no understanding of where the spark of genius came from – she doesn't understand the problem, the user or how the solution came about.

The heat is on. You have 30 seconds to pitch the idea. In an elevator. You smash it: the deal is done! Your pitch lands you a promotion, your boss loses her job, and as a further humiliation, her boyfriend exclaims his love for you and makes you a packed lunch for your first day in your new role.

OK, it's the closing scene to the 1988 film classic *Working Girl,* starring Melanie Griffith as our plucky ideas maker, Sigourney Weaver as her scheming boss, and Harrison Ford as the lunch-making love interest. Although the film has dated, especially in its portrayal of women at work and the trustworthiness of two-timing boyfriends, the fear of someone stealing your idea has not faded.

Take heart, in life, as in filmic Manhattan skyscrapers, your idea is yours. It comes from your life and research; only you can explain how it came about and why you care about making it happen.

People often debate whether to share concepts in case someone steals them. I believe that the more you share, the better you get at explaining it, the more feedback you'll gather, and the better your idea will become. There is so much effort involved in making ideas happen that someone is very unlikely to pinch it. The benefits of sharing are far greater than the risks of keeping schtum.

Communicating your idea is essential to its growth and development. You need to be able to convince people to help you build, use and perhaps fund it. In the startup world there's a do-or-die attitude to pitching, but effective communication isn't a gladiatorial competition: it's about being authentic.

Whether or not you dip your toe in the shark tank or venture into the dragons' den, being able to share ideas authentically and persuasively will advance all areas of your life. The confidence to speak up in meetings and persuade your boss to give you a pay rise will boost your career. The ability to communicate purposefully will also help you to network, meet friends, build communities, and woo partners and their sceptical parents.

Later on, you'll test features with real users and ask them for money, but for now, you are going to share your basic prototype with a few friendly people, who can give you initial feedback and encouragement.

Even if you've only just come up with an idea, saying it out loud will make it more concrete. Let's learn to 'pitch'.

PITCH IT!

When I do workshops I get people to write and deliver a pitch as soon as they have chosen an idea. It's never too early to start sharing – you have an idea, it's got a name, and has been written into a concept and made into a prototype.

It's a small step to turn all that into a written pitch. But delivering a good pitch takes time and practice.

Let's separate the two parts – the words and the performance.

The perfect elevator pitch is clear, simple and memorable. It should be short enough to give in an elevator ride of 30 seconds, just like Melanie Griffith's character Tess does at the end of *Working Girl*.

An elevator pitch is designed to persuade. So, take the elements of your written concept – problem, solution, and benefits – and sell them. At this early stage you're just getting people to understand what your idea is – you don't actually have to sell, so no need to get the fear.

Grab your concept and think of a way to introduce it to your audience. Tried and tested approaches to engage the audience at the beginning include asking a question or telling a story: perhaps how you came up with the idea; how you or someone else experiences the problem; what's special about your idea; or why you're the best person to deliver it.

Next, grab your prototype. Using a prototype as part of your pitch gives you a prompt to remind you what to say, keeps you focussed and stops you fidgeting. It's a prop, not a fully working product – so use it to help your performance. Think about how it can bring your idea to life.

Now that you've got some notes or a mind map of your pitch, let's tackle the performance.

ENGAGE YOUR AUDIENCE

The first audience for author-entrepreneur Tim Ferriss were three chihuahuas.

In March 2007, he was due to present his book *The 4-Hour Work Week* to an audience of tech and creative entrepreneurs at the SXSW Conference.[39] Ferriss was staying with a friend and was nervous. He needed to rehearse, but his friend was at work, so Ferriss practised in front of his friend's dogs instead.

They were a tough audience: if he didn't keep them engaged, they wandered off or lay down and went to sleep. They didn't give a damn about the content or slides – what they cared about was how he spoke and what he did with his hands.

When you pitch, wherever possible, watch how people respond. Like dogs, when do people's ears prick up? What gets them nodding in agreement, smiling, laughing, wagging their tails? These signals will show whether your idea has landed. If people pick up their phones or start talking to a friend, consider their attention lost.

As you develop your idea you'll share it with many different audiences. The first time might be with your mates down the pub, or your gran over tea and ginger biscuits. Your pitch will change when you share it with customers (more on this in Chapter 7) or with accelerators or investors (who you'll find out about in Chapter 12). Each audience will require different content and emphasis. First, let's cover the basics.

CONFIDENCE STARTS WITH THE BODY

Human beings have evolved to judge people's body language – what we see is as important as what we hear. That means your pitch isn't just what you say, but how you say it. A successful pitch needs to project trust and authenticity.

Mariana Marquez co-founded Metaspeech to train startup founders to pitch. 'Confidence,' she says, 'comes across through our bodies when we are grounded and clear in what we say.' She uses her experience as a choreographer alongside knowledge of psychology and physiology to help people use movement and gestures to reinforce their message.

There's an area of research called 'embodied cognition' which looks at how the body can influence the mind. In a famous experiment, participants were split into two groups: the first held a pencil between their teeth, forcing the facial muscles to smile; the second group held a pencil between their upper lip and nose, which created a frown.[40] The 'smilers' were found to react to pleasant sentences much faster than unpleasant sentences – the reverse was true for the 'frowners'. The body led the mind.

There's truth in 'fake it till you make it'. Amy Cuddy's TED Talk on the 'power pose' – how standing confidently will make you feel confident – has been watched by over 50 million people, and legions of fans testify that it works.[41] Try it: stand up straight, legs apart, hands on hips, breathe and feel the power of the pose. You are Wonder Woman.

Cuddy advises that you pose in private before your talk, but taking a strong stance when speaking also projects confidence to your audience.

'For communication to work,' Marquez says, 'for you to really connect with an audience, with an investor, or with your team, you need to be fully present and be yourself. If you are not, then the communication won't be impactful or inspiring.'

Pitching is not about having oodles of confidence or being an extrovert, it's about being authentic. Marquez explains: 'Because our bodies never lie and are completely transparent, whatever we're saying, our bodies are either backing our words or not.' She recommends using gestures to create emphasis and engagement, but make sure they are appropriate to you and not an exaggerated performance.

Practise what you say, and how you say it.

One tip, mortifying as it is, is to film yourself, and watch how you stand, and move your body and hands. Find a few movements that feel like you and use them, sparingly, for emphasis – no wandering all over the place and fist pumping, unless that's your natural style.

HOW TO SHARE YOUR STORY

You've got a basic prototype, you've drafted your pitch and have practised delivering it. It's time to tell your story. These nine steps summarise everything you need to craft your story, build confidence, share your idea and gather feedback.

Step 1: Audience

Consider who you are sharing your prototype with. Think about what problem you are solving for them. Go back to your empathy maps or personas and put yourself in their shoes – imagine how they think and feel – and how you can help them. Finally, think about how they might change after seeing or engaging with your prototype.

Step 2: Story

Next, think about what you're going to tell them. Get creative and tell a story or act out a sketch so as to engage people and spark their interest. But don't oversell your idea – at this stage your focus is gathering feedback, not closing deals. Use your prototype as a prop to explain your concept and bring it to life.

Step 3: Practise

Practise what you're going to say and do. If you're feeling scared of taking your idea into the world, test it out on a friend first; don't ask for feedback on the *idea*, but on *how you share it*. Do this is in a safe space, with someone who you trust and who will give you relevant feedback – you don't want your dad telling you to cut your hair and stop slouching.

Step 4: Get out there!

Get your prototype in front of people. It's OK to start with a few friends as you build confidence but they must be in your target audience. Then, find people you don't know. You know who you're trying to reach so figure out where they are and go there. If you're testing an idea with students, don't seek them out on campus in the summer holiday (yes, I've made this mistake myself).

Step 5: Invite feedback

This is the most important part: welcome people's responses. Ask open questions, get them to describe what they see, feel, think – then ask why. If you receive negative feedback, don't leap to defend your idea, just ask another question and find out their reasons. Staying curious will enable you to turn it into constructive criticism.

Step 6: Listen

Listen carefully to what people say and watch their body language: are they excited and curious, or are they confused and bored?

Step 7: Gather

Consider how you'll gather feedback – by yourself or will you have another person to help? Can they make notes for you, take photos or film? (Remember to get people's permission.) Set aside time to make notes afterwards. Record your observations and key takeaways. You'll use these to review and plan next steps.

Step 8: Be grateful

Thank people for their feedback. Thank your critics as you thank your fans – you will learn from both. Actually, you'll learn more from the critics, so pay particular attention to what they say.

Step 9: Experiment

Play around with how you present your idea: test out different approaches, and develop your story. You'll make mistakes, but use them as an opportunity to learn and improve. Over time you'll share several different ideas and prototypes, so enjoy the process, relish going out and getting feedback – it's a gift that will help you to improve your idea and get more people to love what you are doing.

MAKE IT A CONVERSATION

Nicole Raby had no excuses – she had an idea for an app that helped students find events on campus, and being at university she was surrounded by thousands of people in her target market. All she needed was to ask what they thought.

She started with her friends. That gave her confidence; she could practice what to say and their positive reaction spurred her on to pitch to others.

Raby opened by asking a question: 'Do you know what's happening on campus today?' This conversational starter led naturally into her asking more questions, and then presenting the app prototype and pitching the concept. Because she had framed it as a conversation, the feedback she received gave her new ideas for features – for example, people asked for university building locations and directions.

She quickly found out what didn't resonate too, in particular a 'find your friends' feature. Plus, she discovered that one segment of her target market just didn't like the app. Raby had reckoned that international students would find it useful as they adjusted to life in a new country, but they were less keen than home students – that was definitely something to explore further.

The purpose of getting early-stage feedback on your concept is to help you decide what to do next, just as Raby identified one or two things she didn't expect, which helped her hone her features and target market. In the following chapter, you'll build some real features, to test what actually works for your audience.

FIGURING OUT WHAT IT ALL MEANS: HOW TO EVALUATE FEEDBACK

You've pitched your concept to a few people and gathered feedback, now you need to figure out what it all means.

You might have pages of scribbled notes and observations, voice recordings, and pro-forma sheets with notes written in response to a list of prompts, if you've been organised and enlisted friends to help. If your prototype was online, like a blog, video or Facebook post, your feedback might be in the form of comments, direct messages, tweets or emails.

It might feel like a mess, and it's very easy to get analysis paralysis, worrying what it all means and which bits matter. But you've got this.

Set aside some time. Gather all your findings, tool up with some Post-it notes and pens, make a cup of tea, grab a snack and you're good to go.

Work your way through everything, writing each piece of feedback on a separate Post-it note. Quote exactly the words that people used, so you're not interpreting. If you've got a range of feedback types, you could colour code them using different coloured Post-it notes or pens – say yellow for direct quotes, blue for observations. Don't worry about doing anything with them yet – just note everything down.

When you have a pile of brightly-coloured stickies, containing all your feedback and observations, find a wall and cluster notes with similar feedback together. You don't need a system yet – the feedback will lead you.

When you've got everything on the wall, step back and observe. Take time to look for themes and patterns.

Move things around, sub-divide and organise further. You might have a cluster of positive comments and one of negative responses. More likely, you will have random feedback, with people expressing preferences for colours, shapes and sizes – things that are hard to compare. In that case, prioritise them based on frequency and volume of feedback, and also on strength of feeling.

Tally things up, add labels to the clusters, and mark up the strong opinions so they stand out – you might find that there aren't that many, but that the people who really love or hate your idea focus on similar things.

What's the feedback telling you? Is there anything surprising? Can you draw any conclusions, or does the feedback raise questions you need to explore further? If there are a lot of things to work on, write them all down, prioritise, and then identify just one action to take next. Wrap up your evaluation session by taking photos of your clusters so you can refer to them later.

REFINING YOUR PROTOTYPE

When James Routledge blogged about his anxiety, he didn't know it, but he had made a classic prototype – a quick-to-produce, cheap proof of concept that got people's attention. It wasn't a product or a service and would never be sold. Yet the response he received motivated him and his co-founder George Bettany to build Sanctus.

That blog was a first small step that got an idea about mental health startups into the world so people could engage with it. It generated huge amounts of feedback in emails and direct messages. People also asked what they were going to do next. Bettany said, 'We just followed what people wanted.' That started with setting up a safe space for people to meet and talk. He explains:

'People from all different walks of life would come in on a Wednesday night. It was a safe, impartial, confidential space – that kind of vibe where you could bring anything that you wanted to bring. People valued having this, and that is where the name Sanctus comes from, a sanctuary where we weren't their boss, weren't a colleague, weren't a friend, and you could just talk about anything. And that was, to be honest, without knowing it, our first product or service.'

Over 300 people came to the group sessions in London's Silicon Roundabout, which proved both that there was a problem to solve and that they had the beginnings of a solution.

That's all you need, a small first step, a best guess on what your concept might look like – a prototype that makes a leap from the imagined to the real. Once you've built something, however small, however messy, you can get people to interact with it and give you feedback on what to do next. Read on to find out how to build some real features and get testing.

CHAPTER SUMMARY

- **In short**: Get out there with your prototype and gather feedback.

- **Start now**: Write a 30-second elevator pitch.

- **Go expert**: Pitch like a pro, take a power pose, add movement and gesture.

- **Be happy**: Ask a few friendly faces what they think.

- **Next step**: Create a testable version of your concept and gather some data.

CHAPTER SEVEN

Test

Eight-year-old Alice loved reading, and, luckily for her, her dad Nigel worked for a publishing company. One day when he got home from work, he gave her a chapter of a new book to read. He recalls: 'She came down from her room an hour later glowing, saying, "Dad, this is so much better than anything else." She nagged and nagged me in the following months, wanting to see what came next.'[42]

What came next changed publishing forever, influenced an entire generation, and created the first female author to become a billionaire. Because Alice wanted to read some more.

Alice was given the first draft of *Harry Potter and the Philosopher's Stone*, written by first-time author J.K. Rowling. Her dad was Nigel Newton, chief executive of Bloomsbury Publishing, one of the many publishing companies that were sent that chapter. All the others rejected it.

Newton did something different in giving the chapter to Alice. He tested it with the target market, the sort of person who would read the Harry Potter series.

WHY TEST WITH END USERS?

'I'm actually sad that this question has to even be asked,' says Dave Gray, founder of design business consultancy XPLANE and creator of empathy maps. 'Because products and services are used by users, and if you don't get their opinion, you're going to make a crap product or a crap service.'

I had asked him why we should keep our audience in mind when making products. He's right, if you want to make a good product or service, you must get feedback from your audience. And we're not talking about feedback from friends and family (yes, I know I said it was OK in the last chapter, but we're getting serious now); you need to get it in front of people like Alice, your target market.

Gray explains: 'It's going to be users who judge your performance. The user is essentially the one person that has to be happy and is absolutely the most important person that you need to focus on when you're designing a product or service.'

Gray has spent his whole career helping people to keep their users happy, and he advocates testing with people throughout the development process. He says: 'Get your ideas in front of people as quickly as possible and as early as possible, so you can get their feedback, and you can learn from what they tell you, to start developing something that's better than what you could ever have imagined on your own.'

It can be daunting testing with real users. Gray's advice to build confidence is to take it step by step: 'Take steps incrementally, but try and focus on making things happen, not the busywork like the spreadsheets and the business plans that keep you busy but don't actually teach you anything. You won't learn anything until you start having contact with potential customers.'

You've taken the first step and shared your concept with people. You've gathered feedback, analysed it and have a few thoughts about what to do next. Now we're going to build some features and get people to *test* them – for real, not just giving their opinion on your pitch and prototype.

It's very easy to fall in love with your own idea. But for other people to fall in love with it, they need to use it. That's what this chapter is all about, making something for your target audience to use. You'll learn:

- What a minimal viable product is and how to build one.

- How to take an attitude of experimentation.

- What user testing is and how to test with people.

- A five-day approach to building and testing.

FROM PROPS TO PRODUCT – STEPPING UP TO AN MVP

In the last couple of chapters, we've had fun building and sharing our prototypes; now we need to get our heads around the 'MVP' – a minimum viable product.

A prototype is not the same as an MVP, although they are similar. A prototype is quick and cheap to produce and is often discarded (unless you've got attached to your tinfoil robot). Its purpose is a proof of concept; it gives you a peek at how people might interact with your idea, but it will never be sold, nor make it to the market. You use it as a prop to share your concept and to gather initial feedback.

An MVP is a product which has just enough features to satisfy users, while providing feedback for future development. The concept was popularised by creator of the Lean Startup methodology Eric Ries, who defines it as: '... that version of a new product a team uses to collect the maximum amount of validated learning about customers with the least effort.'[43]

One way to look at the difference between the two is that a prototype shows what your concept is, and MVP asks whether people want it.

As an early or simple version of the product, an MVP reduces time and effort, and creates a springboard for next steps. However, that doesn't mean that it's easy to do. In fact, Ries talks of how he grappled with the concept of an MVP for many years, and he says that doing them well can be difficult. The hard work is in figuring out what is minimum, while still being viable. There is still time and effort required in talking to users and testing the MVP, but much less than building a full product.

WHAT IS MINIMUM *AND* VIABLE?

There is some debate about what 'minimum' means. For some, it's about customers being willing to pay for it; for others, it's about working features; whereas some people want to know if a product has sufficient demand. Let's consult Ries, who gives an example in his blog, Startup Lessons Learned, of when he spent two weeks building a particular feature that 'absolutely nobody wanted'. Looking back on that experience, he realised people could have found out about that feature much sooner if he had run an online advertising campaign on Google and measured engagement.

Creating an ad campaign takes a lot less time, effort and money than coding features; yet, as Ries says, it gets the same answer to the question: 'Do people want this?' That's minimum.

To understand 'viable', we're going to make a wedding cake. This wedding cake is going to be a showstopping, multi-tiered, iced extravaganza. It's complicated and time consuming to make, but how do you know if it's any good, if the happy couple will like it, let alone their tricky future in-laws? You know by making a minimum viable cake.

The cake model of product strategy comes from Brandon Schauer, CEO of design events company Adaptive Path.[44] He describes two approaches: making a dry cake and making a cupcake. Both are *minimum* cakes, but only the cupcake is *viable*.

Why? If you make a basic cake with no icing, fillings or flavours, it's dry and unpalatable, and you can't see what the decorations will look like. It might be minimum, but no one is going to want to eat your cake or feel proud of it at their wedding reception. The feedback to this MVP will be a resounding 'no'.

You abandon your cake. Your vision has died before you even got to share its winning features.

However, if you bake a cupcake – a small version of a wedding cake – with sponge and filling and frosting and sprinkles, then you can get people to taste all the flavour elements, and see your ideas for decoration. It's a cake that you can test, and then iterate and improve. The feedback will help you go on to create a bigger, better version.

DRY CAKE   CUPCAKE

SEEKING PROOF OF CONCEPT

In Chapter 3 we found out how buying a cup of coffee fired up Charlotte Cramer to solve the problem of donor fatigue and uncertainty towards the homeless. She set up CRACK + CIDER with her friend and co-founder Scarlett Montanaro with the ambitious vision of running an IKEA-sized warehouse and distribution network for every item needed by people experiencing homelessness. Tackling the homelessness crisis is a big problem in need of a big solution, but first they had to prove the concept.

They started making plans for an MVP. 'In order for us to launch this,' Cramer says, 'we would have to make it far more simple. We talked about how the complexity was paralysing, and the simplicity was catalysing, and how by boiling everything down to the simplest can enable us to make something happen.'

Raring to go, they brainstormed ways of making it happen. Staying true to their founding moment, when they had decided to spend their money buying coffee rather than on a guy begging in Berlin, they decided to sell coffee out of the back of Cramer's car to raise the funds for items for the homeless. It sounded perfect: it was simple, achievable and true to their origin story.

It never happened.

Most of us freeze when confronted by a big vision. It's such a huge leap to make it happen, which is why the concept of doing something small is incredibly galvanising. But for Cramer and Montanaro, just selling coffee was so small that they were underwhelmed and lost their motivation to act.

They needed a Goldilocks MVP – not too big, not too small, but just right. 'It was a case of balancing,' says Cramer. 'We need proof of concept, but we also need something that we're motivated and excited by, and that feels tangible and interesting. And selling coffees out of the back of the car, we couldn't be bothered to do it, because it felt boring.'

As Ries says about MVPs, it takes time to figure them out – and it took Cramer and her co-founder nearly six months to come up with a second concept to test. They decided to launch a shop; they kept it minimum by only having five products, using existing infrastructure and not paying upfront for stock or storage. Once the concept was agreed, they were offered a venue for a pop-up shop and soon they had the accountability to make it happen.

They opened the shop in the second week of November 2015 for six weeks until the end of December. The tight timescale, combined with the financial constraints, kept them excited, motivated and allowed them to evaluate their concept at the end of the test.

It was a success. They continued to grow CRACK +CIDER, setting up outlets in London, San Francisco and other cities. Looking back, Cramer has this to say about finding the right MVP:

> 'Often, we're told to simplify things, and we confuse that with making things easy. I think people are so rarely challenged, and being challenged is a great motivator, so the fact that it was so easy [to sell coffee] meant that it wasn't motivating to us. The coffee idea was testing the concept, whereas what we really wanted to do was a simplified, cheap version of our big vision.'

Cramer's advice when deciding on the right MVP for you is to find something that:

- Makes the vision actionable.

- Tests the core concept of your idea.

- Stays true to your own principles, values and ambitions.

TESTING A NON-TECH MVP

While the concept of an MVP is rooted in software development, you can apply it to any type of business.

Think back to Alice reading *Harry Potter and the Philosopher's Stone* – she was reading sample chapters, not feeding back on the pitch for the book, the cover, or the concept of a wizard at boarding school.

In the last chapter, we met Mariana Marquez of Metaspeech, who gave us body confidence to pitch our ideas. A few years ago, she was on maternity leave and in the same position as you, working on an early idea. 'I had two kids, one was a baby,' Marquez says, 'when I got to be part of something called Campus for Moms at Google Campus. You could take your baby to the once a week classes on branding and how to grow your tech business – except, I didn't have a tech business.'

She wasn't planning on launching a startup, but wanted to draw on her skills as a choreographer and dancer. Being in an environment surrounded by tech business founders, she saw that they often lacked the skills to share their ideas. She had a hunch that her dance training might be valuable; she just needed to try it out.

The MVP for what would later become Metaspeech was an advert: 'Sign up for a free workshop.' Google Campus promoted it on social media and hosted the workshop. Marquez and her co-founder Emma Zangs got 30 sign-ups and ran her first workshop. She continued to host and advertise more events, using Eventbrite to manage bookings.

Over the next three months, the workshops grew to over 100 people attending. Her concept was validated. The approach of testing each iteration stayed with her and Zangs as they developed new products and services, such as one-to-one training, corporate workshops and online courses.

BRAINSTORMING YOUR TESTABLE MVP

Let's figure out what's both minimum and viable for your concept. While I usually urge you to do things as quickly as possible – you built a prototype in an hour, and set yourself a challenging goal for a 24-hour hackathon – now, time is your friend. Step back and consider your options. Find your creative hotspot, take a walk by the sea, go for a run on a hill, or swim in a lake to mull over those options.

One tip is to set a time limit for how long you'll consider an idea. Professor Frank Partnoy has studied the beneficial effects of time on decision making and he found that waiting helps.[45] Waiting isn't procrastination – there's an optimal time to act. Professor Partnoy's advice is to agree in advance how long you'll take to decide. So, set yourself a deadline and use that time to figure out the best MVP.

Start just as you did for a prototype, by brainstorming different ways you might build a testable MVP. Keep it as small as possible, but feasible so it tests something specific – for example, whether a part of it works, if there's demand, or if people will pay.

Go back to the feedback on your prototype. What did you learn? Was there a something people really liked about the concept? Can you build that into an MVP? For example, you might make a concierge product to see how you can deliver a service or an advertising campaign linked to a landing page that measures click-through rates.

Don't think about the big vision for what it could eventually be. Think cupcake: small, easy to make and includes core elements of the concept.

1, 2, 3. TESTING, TESTING, TESTING

Testing will give you the chance to improve your initial concept and will decrease the risk of it failing. There are three principles of testing to keep in mind:

- Test early.

- Test often.

- Test with end users.

Testing early saves time and money as you validate decisions earlier, and testing often enables you to iterate and improve so you keep moving in the right direction. And it goes without saying that you should test with end users to validate your assumptions. Always remember: *you are not your user.*

So, how do you go about testing? Let's go back to Eric Ries' mistake when his team spent weeks coding unwanted new product features. He learnt that he could have tested that assumption faster and more cheaply by running a Google AdWords campaign to check if there was demand from users. Let's look at how someone else did it.

STEMETTES – IT'S ALL ABOUT EXPERIMENTING

Anne-Marie Imafidon was working full-time for Deutsche Bank when she realised how under-represented women were in technology jobs. The problem was stark, and Imafidon was determined to find a solution, so she started the Stemettes Project to inspire girls to study science, technology, engineering and maths, and give them a chance of STEM career success.

In Chapter 5, we heard about the magic Imafidon created by buying a domain and putting her idea into the world. Her process was to gather feedback by 'working out loud' – sharing her thoughts as she researched the problem by writing blogs and learning from the feedback as her idea took shape.

She reached a point where she had a solution to test: 'I wrote a separate blog,' Imafidon says, 'about what I proposed to do, talking about the solution and what we were working on and planning. I was like, "Let's test this and see where this goes."'

Imafidon decided to run a launch event. Her background in science gave her experience running experiments. Imafidon pulled on her metaphorical lab coat and goggles and got to work on a hypothesis. A scientist will observe something and use that evidence to change the hypothesis and test again.

'When you do an experiment,' she says, 'you sit and you watch and you take notes on what's happening, how it's happening, how much it's happening. And if something goes wrong, it's not because I'm a failure. It's because maybe that element of that experiment wasn't set up right.'

Imafidon received feedback from the launch event that it was too informal, so she changed it for the next event. The feedback on that was: 'No we liked how it was at the launch.' She compared the two experiments and decided the original hypothesis of having a fun informal event worked better, so she switched back to the original format. It's hard when you make a mistake, but it's part of a process of iteration that makes ideas better.

Taking an experimental approach taught Imafidon and her team what worked and helped them develop the central proposition of Stemettes based around their audience's needs and wants. She says:

> 'Fun and informality is core to what we do because we know that's something the girls like, something that works, something that adds to the impact. That's just one example of iterating. Our first event was a mid-week evening, which is not great if you want younger people [to attend] who have early bedtimes. So now, we don't do too late, and we don't do weekdays. All those kinds of things you keep picking up on; you're constantly observing.'

Years on, Stemettes still experiments. It's important for Imafidon to create a culture where staff can try things out. Whoever you are, however old, and with whatever experience, you have something to contribute.

Like Imafidon, make like a scientist and keep experimenting, testing your ideas and learning from the results. And remember the three rules of testing: test early, test often and test with end users.

USER TESTING

'Giving your design a critical review is difficult. It's like trying to edit your own article. You often read what you meant, not what you actually wrote.'

Jennifer Aldrich's work at InVision, a platform for digital product design, is all about creating simple and intuitive customer experiences. While she's an expert in reviewing designs, her opinion isn't what matters. Aldrich says, 'you are not your user', meaning that to properly test something, you need to get your audience involved. That's where user testing comes in.

User testing is found in digital product development, where prototypes, MVPs, new products and features are tested in a structured way. It's a moderated test where a 'user', someone in your target audience, is set a series of tasks and is observed doing them. The tester might be given a task – for example, on a shopping website they might be asked to choose a pair of trainers in their size and add them to the shopping basket.

While user tests are often run by professional user experience researchers, they are easy to organise and run yourself, and they work for all types of concepts, products and services – think of taste tests for food and drink. But before we get to that, listen to Aldrich describe her first user test:

> 'It was being conducted in another room and broadcast into a conference room where our design team was sitting. The tester was really struggling with a task, and we were all basically leaning sideways saying: "RIGHT! It's to the right! It's right THERE!" And she couldn't find the call to action at all.'

Users tests are set up so the person testing the design is in one room and the observers are in another. There is a facilitator in the room with the tester, but they cannot intervene – think of it like being a wildlife photographer whose job is to take photos of the starving polar bears – under no circumstances can you give them food which might save their lives. Aldrich reflects:

> 'It was incredibly frustrating, and made us realise that something so obvious to us when we

designed the screen was completely invisible and confusing to her as a user without previous knowledge or background on the design. The same issue happened with the testers that followed. We thought we'd been so thorough, that the product would be dead simple, but it wasn't. It was really eye opening for me.'

It's not easy watching someone completely fail to do the one thing you want them to do, the thing that might solve their problem and make them happy. But do not, under any circumstance, blame them or tell them what to do – your job in a user test is to observe, learn from what they do and fix it.

HOW TO ORGANISE AND RUN A USER TEST

User testing is big business for digital products and software, but the principle works for all types of ideas. There are logistics involved in getting a test up and running, but like organising any event, the tasks are finite, predictable and repeatable. It gets easier the more you do it. Here's what you need to consider:

Before the test

You need a room. Make sure it is easy to find, clean and set up for your test with a table and chairs.

You need to record what happens. Professional user testing labs will have cameras or two-way mirrors, but you could be in the room observing and making notes, or you could use a voice- or screen-recorder.

When you recruit testers, find a diverse group of people who will be representative of your whole target audience. You're familiar with your audience, so you'll have a good idea how to reach them – you might put up a poster on a noticeboard, a request on a forum or email list, or an advert on social media.

As the testers arrive

It's most efficient to run several tests in a day – usually six to eight people will give consistent results. When people arrive, welcome them and thank them for their time; then brief them on what's involved, and ask for their permission. Be conversational and friendly while also being professional.

Explain that they are there to test the concept – they are not being tested themselves, so there are no wrong answers. You're looking for problems with the concept, so it's good if they get stuck. Tell them that you're keen to hear how they get on, and want them to 'think aloud' and explain what they are doing and thinking.

During the test

Warm your testers up with chit chat, then segue into asking the questions you've prepared. Introduce them to the MVP, explaining what it is, and set them a task – for example, fill in a registration form or chose a meal from the menu.

Don't guide them in what to do and don't lead them with statements like, 'We really love this website and we think you will too.' Don't ask leading questions or ones where the only answers are yes or no – you're looking for explanations.

Do ask deeper questions – lots of why, what, how, when and where questions. For example: What are you looking at? What do you think of that? When did you expect that to happen? Where would you go next? How would you do that? Why?

Observe their body language. Are they confused, frowning, happy or excited?

After the test

At the end of the test, ask follow-up questions. This is the time to step back from the details of what the tester did, to consider the bigger picture, such as their preferences about what they did and didn't like, and what would they improve.

It does seem like a lot of work, but the results will transform your thinking and give you concrete ways to improve.

If you don't have the time to do an in-person test, scale back. For example, you could stop people in the street and ask them to test something; or, if you have a digital MVP, you could test it over Skype with a screenshare or automatic screen-recording, using one of the many online tools available.

WORKING WITH YOUR USERS

In Chapter 2, Dr Al-Ubaydli told us: 'You have to sit with the users in the front line.' At the beginning of his career this was about empathy, working with his medical colleagues to help solve their problems. This approach stayed with him as he built Patients Know Best, medical records owned and controlled by the patient.

He had two types of users – clinicians and patients, who had very different needs and wants – which meant that he had to test with both. He described the process of testing as 'powerful', not only because he was fixing things they spotted, but because he got to understand their motivations and then figure out what they needed his product to do longer term. He found out the one or two things they cared about in the next few months. Dr Al-Ubaydli explains:

> 'I sat down with doctors and nurses, and they'd say, "I want [the app] to do that." In a few days' time, having worked with the developers, we'd say: "Look, they've done what you wanted." They loved that cycle of feedback. Then they'd tell their colleagues: "Look at this feature on the screen, I did that."'

For Dr Al-Ubaydli, the process of testing helped improve the service he was offering, but also engaged his first users to become champions for the product and spread the word to colleagues. Recommendations are a brilliant way to grow your audience – you'll find out more about that in Chapter 11.

FIVE DAYS TO BUILD AND TEST AN IDEA

Sometimes your biggest breakthroughs come when you're not actively working on something. Holidays can provide the perfect opportunity to unwind and seek inspiration. Back in 2015, I was lying on a beach in Croatia listening to an early episode of the 'StartUp' podcast.[46] While I was topping up my tan, I heard how the fledgling podcasting startup Gimlet Media got advice from Google Ventures on how to 'fake' an app to test with users.

I wanted some of that 'fake'. Once I'd dusted the sand from my feet and returned to my day job in innovation, I set about implementing the process I had heard about – the Design Sprint.

It started as a one-off experiment, but the results were so successful that over the course of a year I ran a Design Sprint every month. Repeating the process again and again meant that I learnt tons. Granted, I made some mistakes, but the result of that year of sprinting transformed the business I worked for, and gave me valuable skills to use on my side hustle.

The Design Sprint is a simple five-day process created by Jake Knapp at Google Ventures. He calls it 'a greatest hits of business strategy, innovation, behavioural science, design and more'.

It was designed to help startups answer crucial questions through prototyping and testing ideas with customers. The process found fame with the likes of Facebook and Airbnb, and has been used by all sorts of traditional businesses. It works whether you're a large corporate, a scrappy startup or a lone ideas-maker.

Knapp's book *Sprint* outlines the objective of each day, and gives lots of practical advice, case studies and handy checklists of what to do and buy, including suggested snacks.[47] His accompanying blog also features lots of inspiring stories of how people implemented the process.[48]

It's a useful process because it condenses the principles of building and testing into a structured time frame. If you want a schedule to work to – read on.

TINKERING NOT ADVISED

A classic sprint involves a small team of people who work collaboratively to build and test an idea. It follows a strict daily pattern.

Monday creates a path for the week. It starts with agreeing a goal for the sprint and mapping the challenge. By the end of the day, the team can *pick a target problem* to solve over the coming four days.

Tuesday is all about *generating solutions* through sketching ideas. The focus is not artistic ability but critical thinking.

Wednesday kicks off by critiquing all the solutions from the day before and deciding which ones have the best chance of achieving the goal. The *selected solution* gets made into a storyboard.

Thursday the team takes the storyboard and makes it into a realistic *prototype*. That means building something. As time is limited (there's only one day to build) the main principle is: fake it.

Friday is the day the prototype is *put in front of real customers* who will be interviewed and observed using it.

© Jake Knapp, reprinted by permission of the author

Tinkering with the process is not advised as its success lies in constraint. In my experience, although my design sprints had a budget, the teams I worked with preferred a DIY approach to building prototypes and MVPs – to be honest it was more fun to get hands-on and build stuff yourself.

If you've got a problem to solve and no money, then make some time to sprint. You could reduce the length of time spent each day – for example, having an evening-only sprint – but stick to doing the tasks daily to maintain momentum. You might be frazzled by Friday, but you'll have raced ahead with your idea.

RUNNING A MARATHON

Having a hustle is like running a marathon, but that doesn't mean you need to maintain a consistent pace – periods of acceleration, followed by a slow stretch taking in the view, will make your journey more manageable and enjoyable. You might build a prototype in an hour, take a few weeks to decide what your MVP will be, or go all out with a five-day Design Sprint that gets you from identifying a problem on the Monday, to brainstorming and building mid-week, to testing on a Friday.

Also, it's far more fun running a marathon when you have other people cheering you on – testing your idea builds an audience of early users. Back to user testing expert Jennifer Aldrich:

'Starting with a laser focus on your target audience is extremely important. Do your research in advance to identify who you're building the product for, and to understand who they are and what they really need. Conducting usability testing with all of your primary personas throughout the entire design cycle is incredibly important as well – it will save tons of cash in what could turn into costly revamps.'

Testing might feel like a scary thing to do – and you're right, it is – but if you don't get people to use your MVP, you'll never know if it's any good. Next, we're going to step up the testing by asking people to pay.

Be brave, share your idea and give it to people to try – you'll learn so much.

CHAPTER SUMMARY

- **In short**: Testing saves you time and money and makes your idea better.

- **Start now**: Figure out what's minimum and viable to create a testable version of your concept.

- **Go expert**: Take five days to build and test something with a Design Sprint.

- **Find your happy**: Work with users to improve your idea, and find early champions to spread the word.

- **Next step**: The ultimate currency of validation – ask for money.

CHAPTER EIGHT

Validate

Three friends had an idea to make and sell smoothies. They thought the drinks tasted amazing – but amazing enough for them to quit their day jobs and dedicate themselves to smashing up fruit full-time? They decided to validate their hypothesis.

> 'We put up a big sign asking people if they thought we should give up our jobs to make smoothies, and put a bin saying "Yes" and a bin saying "No" in front of the stall. Then we got people to vote with their empties. At the end of the weekend, the "Yes" bin was full, so we resigned from our jobs the next day and got cracking.'[49]

Those three friends were Adam Balon, Richard Reed and Jon Wright, and asking that question in 1999 led to the creation of Innocent Drinks, now owned by Coca-Cola.

The contents of the bins might have been rubbish, but they were data – countable, verifiable data that answered an important question.

VALIDATE ME

You might have been carrying around your idea for years, never quite knowing whether it has genuine possibility. That can be lonely, but now your idea is out in the world you can find proof.

We all need validation. Proof that our idea works, corroboration that it's a good one, confirmation that we should keep going. While feedback from users is essential in honing your idea, you need validation to make it happen.

And you need data to give you validation.[50] As W. Edwards Deming said: 'Without data, you're just another person with an opinion.'

But what counts as data? In philosophy, you use data as the basis for reasoning. That's the definition I like, because the purpose of gathering data is to make an argument – it might be to persuade yourself to continue with an idea, or abandon it, or convince someone to invest in your idea or work with you to build it. Data are facts to back you up as you make a case to continue.

For the founders of Innocent, their data was actual rubbish; for others it might be feedback from user testing, click-through rates on an advert, sign-ups to an email list, or sales. All these data provide external verification of something which has been deeply personal.

And nothing wins an argument more than money, that's why in this chapter you'll:

- Find out what commitment looks like.

- Build confidence to sell your idea.

- Ask people to pay for it.

- Pull everything into a one-page business plan.

HOW TO GATHER DATA FOR VALIDATION

Making an idea happen is like reading a choose-your-own-adventure book. The story has a beginning like any other, but rather than one path through, you find there are multiple options – some will lead you forward, other times you choose a wrong path and start again. Your choices will alter both how your story ends and the time it takes to get there.

My advice is to take small steps and seek validation along your journey, to minimise missteps while building confidence about your direction.

Be patient. Don't rush to build and release something. Instead design a series of incrementally bigger tests.

Take the title of this book. I came up with what I thought was a winning and witty title, but my editor was sceptical; it was a bit of a cliché. She took to Google, gathered a list of other books with the same title (and a romcom starring Jennifer Aniston), and the argument was won – I had to start over.

I built in tests so I could check I was heading in the right direction with a new title. I designed a collaborative brainstorm with my beta readers – a group of trusted experts and people within the target market – to help me generate titles. Together we came up with 59 ideas.

With my editor, we scrutinised the list, evaluating them against the book concept, the market and similar titles (and romcoms starring Jennifer Aniston). Eventually it was whittled down to five titles, which we tested on Google AdWords over a week. There was one clear winner, and as an additional bonus, we found out something about demographics – which age group and region liked it the most.

That two-stage process took a classic divergent to convergent route to choose ideas, which were then validated with quantitative data.

Surveys, like ad campaigns, are a quick, easy and cheap route to get quantitative data to validate your qualitative feedback. Use feedback to create surveys, where people select an opinion that matches what they think or feel. You can run super quick polls on Twitter or Facebook, or knock up surveys on Google forms, then share them on social networks and forums.

The early stages of making something are all about validating, tweaking and improving your idea. However, at some point you need to find out if people are willing to commit.

The question remains: do people *really* want it?

A happy hustle is about taking small steps, not freaking yourself out when you hit something difficult, and trying to find the simplest, easiest way into a task so that you build confidence, keep motivated and enjoy the process. But, sometimes, hustling is just plain hard, and you need to take a big step to move ahead. For many of us, asking people to pay is that hardest big step. Selling might come naturally to a few people, but for many, it's a truly hideous experience. To make it easier, you might decide to sell to a few friendly faces, a mate, a family member, or perhaps your mum.

Bad idea says, Rob Fitzpatrick.

FROM FEEDBACK TO COMMITMENT

'People say you shouldn't ask your mom whether your business is a good idea. That's technically true, but misses the point,' says Fitzpatrick. 'You shouldn't ask *anyone* whether your business is a good idea. At least not in those words. Your mom will lie to you the most (just 'cuz she loves you), but it's a bad question and invites everyone to lie to you at least a little.'[51]

Asking our friends and family is a classic trap that plays into confirmation bias – the tendency to search for information that supports our existing beliefs or hypotheses and to ignore or distort contradictory evidence.

This cognitive bias is played out every day on social media, where people exist in filter bubbles. Take any contentious issue like climate change, gun control, immigration or abortion rights: people seek out views similar to their own; when confronted with opposing facts they become further entrenched in their beliefs; and, even more frightening, they distort facts to support their preconceptions.

It's not just shouty internet trolls who do this – we all do, especially when we're trying to validate an idea. Researchers have found that people test hypotheses in a one-sided way by phrasing questions to get the answers they want to hear. You end up in a situation where you hammer home one option while rejecting all other alternatives.

You can counter confirmation bias by taking an experimental approach to testing ideas and then validating the evidence, deliberately seeking findings that challenge and disprove your beliefs, and determining in advance the criteria you'll use to base your decisions on.

This is what Fitzpatrick advises in his book, *The Mom Test*, based on his own experience as an introverted startup founder who was bad at sales and needed to figure out if his business idea was any good. He says:

'Stop expecting other people to tell you the truth, and instead ask questions that are carefully designed in a way which removes the discomfort and makes it impossible for anyone (even your mom) to lie to you. People always lie with compliments and opinions if you ask them about an idea, but they can't really lie if you ask them for specific, concrete examples of what they did in the past. And then you extrapolate from their existing behaviour to figure out what they might do, in your opinion as an entrepreneur, in the future.'

But there comes a time when insight isn't enough – you need commitment from customers. Fitzpatrick says: 'Commitment can be cash, but it doesn't have to be. Think of it in terms of currency – what are they giving up for you?'

There are three major currencies:

- **Time** – such as asking a customer to do a trial for a significant period or giving feedback on a prototype.

- **Reputation** – asking for an introduction to peers or a senior decision maker, or getting a public case study or testimonial.

- **Financial commitments** – getting a letter of intent, a deposit or pre-order.

The more a customer commits, the more seriously you take what they are saying, and the more valuable the validation.

If you have an idea that solves a problem for people, helps them do something, and brings them some benefit, they will pay for it. It's a hard step to take, asking for financial commitment, but it's easy in the sense that it provides a simple go/no-go indicator. Is this idea worthwhile enough that people are willing to hand over money for it – yes or no?

LEARN TO SELL

Dave Gray of XPLANE agrees with Fitzpatrick, saying the that ultimate commitment is a sale. 'The easiest way to know when people finally get pains and gains,' says Gray, 'is when they buy something.' Learning to sell isn't easy, but it is necessary. If you want to make ideas happen, then just following a passion isn't enough, you must make money. He explains:

> 'Following your heart purely for your own heart's sake only works if you're independently wealthy or extremely committed. You have not only to follow your heart, but establish the things that you care about that are relevant to others, that they are willing to pay for, and you have to develop the skills to be able to provide a service.'

He reckons learning to sell is the number one skill you need: 'If you want to develop some skills, behaviours and attitudes that will help you innovate and influence change, learn how to sell. It's really that simple. Learn how to sell your ideas, because that's what's going to give you the energy to keep going.'

While 'hustling' might have shady undertones, we're talking about 'having a happy hustle' for a reason: you've got to put the work into getting your concept into the world. That means you must persuade, promote and sell your idea and what it can do for people. Only then can you generate income on the side to supplement your salary or make enough to quit your job.

FROM PROTOTYPE TO PAYMENT

My co-founder Chris Smith and I had been playing around with prototypes for writers for years – we had created workshops, webinars, paper trackers, email courses and even basic web apps.

It was such fun building stuff, getting people to test, and gathering feedback. But that was all we were doing, just running small experiments, learning about our users, what problems they had and how we could solve them.

We were stuck in a comfortable feedback loop and never got beyond feedback. We needed commitment. We had to ask for money. When we did, it changed everything.[52]

Here's what happened. We recruited a bunch of people over Facebook and Twitter and challenged them to write a project of their choice over five days. The only rule was that they had to check in with us every 24 hours to tell us what they'd written. If they didn't check in by the deadline, they lost a life. They only had two lives to use – if they used both, they were off the challenge.

The first prototype was email. Day by day, people worked towards their personal, self-directed goals. We stayed up through the night responding to their emails, sending nudges, answering questions and setting them new deadlines – all accompanied by a spreadsheet from hell.

It worked – 55 per cent of people completed the challenge and wrote for five days. We had some awesome feedback and some very grateful people –

many of whom had achieved something they'd never been able to do before.

On to the next step. We decided to automate it, and built a basic digital MVP that replicated what we had done ourselves. There was a simple front end that people used to tell us what they were writing, and this triggered transactional emails – we didn't have to stay up all night to respond to messages.

We started off small, letting in batches of people to ensure the system could cope. In total, 1,127 people signed up. Our completion rates decreased – totally understandable as people will never respond as well to a bot than a human being – but not as much as we feared.

Twenty-five per cent of users stuck with the product over five days and completed the challenge. That's 284 people who wrote something that they might never have written before, by using a fully automated, digital product. We set up a simple satisfaction survey with the classic one question 'Net Promotor Score', and our responses were in the 'excellent' range.[53] We were on to something.

We'd hit this point before – run an experiment, gathered great feedback, solved problems for people – but had always given up because we didn't have the money to build a 'proper' product.

Not this time.

We decided to add in a paywall at the end of the challenge to give users the chance to 'continue' for a one-off payment of £10. We needed to know if there was a market, or if we just had a side project thinking up weird writing challenges for people.

While the paywall was in place, 733 people signed up to the free challenge, and 162 completed the challenge – 22 per cent. But of those 22 per cent who completed, a whacking 71 per cent upgraded and paid. Overall, that's a 16 per cent conversion rate from initial sign-up to paying. People didn't pay us because the product looked pretty (it really didn't), they paid us because it worked for them.

It all feels rather embarrassing to ask people to pay for an MVP. But it's worth it. Our experiment proved that we had found a problem that people were willing to hand over cash to solve – and that our solution helped them. The results got us a place on an accelerator programme, which gave us the money to build the rest of the product.

You need to hold your blushes and start selling. Here's how.

FIND YOUR VALUE PROPOSITION

In Chapter 6 you crafted an elevator pitch to share your concept. It described the problem, its solution and benefits, all wrapped up in a neat name, with a story to tell and a prop to bring it to life. That's the foundation for your sales pitch. Time to level up.

Forget about the stereotypical sales patter used by a shiny-suited second-hand-car salesman, and focus instead on your audience. Yep, we're back to empathy, feeling people's pain and communicating the gains.

Selling something is making a promise to someone – ideally a promise you'll keep. A sales pitch is a value proposition, because you're promising the customer that they will get value from using your product or service.

A value proposition does three things; it explains:

• How your idea solves a problem.

• What benefits people will get from using your idea.

- Why people should use your idea rather than someone else's.

This builds on your elevator pitch. Think of that pitch as explaining the 'what' of your concept, while the value proposition of your sales pitch is the 'why'. You need to explain why someone should buy what you're selling.

Gray explains: 'No one is going to buy anything until they see that there's a gain they can get that solves a pain they have today.' He gives me the example of two guys in a snowstorm to demonstrate the importance of a value proposition.

Imagine the scene: you're in Paris for a conference. It's winter, it's freezing cold, and it has just started snowing. You're tired after a hard day and desperate to get back to the warmth of your hotel, but there are no taxi cabs.

This is the founding story of Uber. There's a pain (cold, snow, lack of taxis), a gain (warm hotel) and a solution (on demand taxi). Plus, it has all the elements of a great story – hell, who cares if it really happened like that, it's got Paris!

If we look at Uber's current value proposition, it sells in the benefits immediately: 'One tap and a car comes directly to you. Hop in – your driver knows exactly where to go. And when you get there, just step out. Payment is completely seamless.'[54]

Because you've been sharing your concept with people, you'll have feedback from your audience to craft a killer value proposition. Grab your pitch from Chapter 5 and consider the feedback you've received. What benefits did people see in your idea? How does that differ from the benefits you originally listed? What is the gain to people if they use it?

Finally, double down on why your concept is better than something already in the market. We'll talk about competition later in the chapter, so you'll soon find out how to consider this more thoroughly.

Let's dust down Nicole Raby's pitch for DiscoverCampus. The long version went like this:

> *DiscoverCampus helps students to quickly and cheaply find the entertainment, food and drink that they love on their university campus. The iPhone and Android app uses GPS location-tracking technology to send students tailored information about the events, outlets and special offers near them that are happening now.*

It covers the first two requirements: explaining how the idea solves a problem and what benefits people will get from using it. But there's work to be done on why students should use her app rather than something else. Luckily, feedback helped her figure this out.

First, by asking questions she found out that students use Google Maps for directions, but while that gets you where you're going, it doesn't tell you what's on in the first place. That's where her app could add value.

Plus, she found out what the gain was to students. While they wanted to make the most of their university experience and not miss out, the real benefit was feeling like part of a community. Raby dug into this a bit more and found some research on how students at campus universities gave higher satisfaction ratings than those at universities where facilities were spread wider across a city. Her goal was to create a tool that made universities feel more inclusive.

You've got your value proposition, now you're ready to go out there and sell, sell, sell. But before you rush out the door and start flogging your wares to the first person you meet, you need to figure out what Gray calls your 'WHODO'.[55] In short, you need to be clear 'who' you are selling to and what you want them to 'do' – this is the specific call to action that they should take.

Take a moment now to write your value proposition, identify your sales target and call to action.

PULLING IT ALL TOGETHER

This is the final chapter on honing your idea. Before we move on to making it happen, you need a plan.

Business plans suck. No one likes writing them, no one likes reading them, and they are out of date the second you print them out. However, they give rigour to your idea and prompt you to find out if anyone is doing anything similar.

There are loads of great templates out there to help pull your hustle together, but many of them are focussed on traditional businesses.

Ash Maurya, CEO of LeanStack, created a quick and easy template for ideas makers to get their thoughts lined up. Inspired by the Lean Startup, he based it on Alex Osterwalder's Business Model Canvas,[56] and called it the Lean Canvas. You can fill in the one-page template in twenty minutes by working through the nine building blocks for your idea, starting with the problem you're trying to solve.

'My main objective with Lean Canvas,' says Maurya, 'was making it as actionable as possible while staying entrepreneur-focussed. The metaphor I had in mind was that of a grounds-up tactical plan or blueprint that guided the entrepreneur as they navigated their way from ideation to building a successful startup.'[57]

Print out a copy of the Lean Canvas[58] and fill in as many of the boxes as possible now, and, I promise, by the end of this book, you'll have the canvas complete.

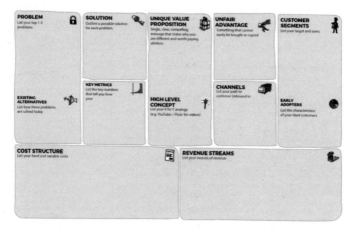

© LeanStack, reprinted with permission from Ash Maurya. Lean Canvas is adapted from The Business Model Canvas and is licensed under the Creative Commons Attribution-Share Alike 3.0 Un-ported License.

Using the canvas, make notes on:

- **Problem**. List your top one to three problems, and their existing alternatives: how these problems are solved today.

- **Solution**. Outline a possible solution for each problem.

- **Key metrics**. List the numbers that tell you how your business is doing.

- **Unique value proposition**. Write a single clear compelling message that turns an unaware visitor into an interested prospect.

- **Unfair advantage**. Note what it is about your idea that cannot be easily bought or copied.

- **Channels**. List your paths to customers.

- **Customer segments**. List your target customers and users.

- **Cost structure**. List your fixed and variable costs.

- **Revenue streams.** List your sources of revenue.

If you can't complete all the sections – metrics and cost structure will be tricky at this stage – make notes on how you'll get these figures in the future, rather than leaving blanks.

WHAT ABOUT COMPETITION?

Maurya excluded competition from the Lean Canvas, instead focussing on how customers deal with their problems today in the 'existing alternatives' section. He says: 'Your true competition is not who *you* think they are, but who your customers think they are.'

Every idea has a competitor, and so will yours.

Follow Maurya's advice and dig through your feedback to see what your target customers do already. There's a famous example that the competition for a McDonald's milkshake isn't Burger King's milkshake but bananas, donuts, bagels, coffee and Snickers bars.[59] Competition isn't another brand in the same space, but for McDonald's it's everything that goes into someone's stomach. In the same way, the competition for Netflix isn't other TV streaming sites, but how people spend their leisure time.

Think back to Rob Fitzpatrick's rule for the Mom Test – encouraging people to talk about specific concrete examples of what they did in the past, you'll find out who your competition really is.

After you've gone through your feedback, you need to do some desk research – in other words, hit search on Google or YouTube.

You need some way to log what you find, so set up a spreadsheet. In the first column, write the names of ten to twenty competitors, and include other headings like their domain, social media accounts, value proposition, products, audience, prices – whatever you might learn from.

Bonus tip: once you've logged the key areas of comparison, why not rank competitors on how well they do in these areas? For example, if they have a brilliant website landing page, give that a score of ten. That way you can sort out who does what well, or you can total the scores across key areas to see who your biggest competitor is.

It's valuable doing a competitor analysis at this stage because having competition validates that you have a problem worth solving. If there is no competition, you'll struggle to get support, as you'll be so early to market that no one will believe you're onto something. Go on, find out who else is there.

MAKE AMAZING THINGS HAPPEN

'All around us in nature and in life, things are being created all the time, new and beautiful and amazing things,' says Dave Gray. 'If you want to actually learn how to do that, start with learning how to sell, because nothing happens until somebody sells something. This is what empathy, and pains and gains, and all those things are about. If you want to control your destiny, learn how to make change happen instead of waiting for it to happen by itself.'

You've asked people for feedback on your early prototype, sold an MVP for real money, gathered data and evaluated it, and finally, you've pulled all that together into a business plan that positions you in the market. Now it's time to get comfortable with failure and build the resilience you need to make your idea happen.

CHAPTER SUMMARY

- **In short**: Sell your idea to people and get validation to continue.

- **Start now**: Figure out what commitment you need from people to prove they really want what you're offering.

- **Go expert**: Create a one-page business plan and find out who else is already in the market.

- **Be happy**: Get your hustle on and make some cash.

- **Next step**: Embrace failure and learn from your mistakes.

3 Making ideas happen

9 FAIL
reflect
growth mindset
learn
rejoice

10 PIVOT
Quit
Pivot
Persevere
fail better
how to pivot

11 GROW
community
product market fit
Metrics
AARRR!

12 HUSTLE
Side hustle or startup?
Investment

HAPPY
YAY
build a support network
GRIT
flourish
ask for help!

CHAPTER NINE

Fail

Carolina Martins was in a party mood. She'd just stepped off the plane from Brazil, her homeland, which was hosting the 2014 World Cup. It was her first day in Silicon Valley. She'd won a place at the prestigious Singularity University and walked onto the NASA Campus feeling happy, curious and ready to play. She was immediately knocked out of her comfort zone.

Martins was greeted with the usual chit-chat opener of: 'What do you do?' When she explained her challenging, high-powered, highly-paid role in corporate innovation, the conversational follow up was: 'And what else?' What had got her there was no longer enough. She needed to do more – much, much more.

Everything about the Singularity University Global Solutions Programme is designed to stretch you. With the goal of developing solutions to problems that will affect a billion people over the next ten years, you need to be bold. Failure is an inevitable part of the process.

AN EXERCISE IN FAILURE

In one of the first exercises, the students were sent into the streets and told to rack up as many failures as they could in a couple of hours. Martins rose to the challenge and asked if she could eat people's French fries, if they would sing a song with her, give her a ride.

The challenge taught her two things:

1. It's surprising how often you succeed, even when you set out to fail.

2. When you do fail, it's not that bad – you just try again.

Over the following ten weeks, Martins overcame her fears. After finishing the programme she quit her job, sold her flat, moved continents and started from scratch – not something she had expected to do in her mid-thirties.

Failure is the ultimate 'f' word. The path to hustle success contains many obstacles that can knock you off course. Embrace this and stop a fear of failure holding you back. You'll do this by developing a growth mindset in which you reframe failure as learning. This chapter will inspire you to be bold, and it will give you the tools to evaluate what has happened when you fail, and the strength to pick yourself back up again.

The best way to avoid failure is to not try. Martins realised she was operating at a level below her capabilities. She says: 'Before I went in, I had these glorified ideas of entrepreneurship and of those gifted individuals who build amazing things. But the lesson for me was: the only reason why I haven't done it is because I haven't tried.'

By the time she left, Martins had the self-confidence to believe that everything is possible – it's just a question of trying and doing it.

By overcoming setbacks, you and your ideas become stronger. There's a saying in innovation: 'Fail often to succeed earlier.' It's better to make mistakes early in the life of your idea, when they're smaller and quicker to recover from. In other words, fail fast.

It's time to fail. Over the coming chapter, you'll learn to be fearless, and:

- Find out why failure is necessary.

- Build, measure, learn – the Lean Startup way.

- Reflect on what has happened and take time to celebrate.

- Develop a growth mindset by learning how to learn.

FAILURE IS PART OF THE PROCESS

Failing is hard, and it hurts like hell. Unfortunately, if you're launching a product, service or business, it's likely you're going to stumble and fall along the way – often in public.

Believe me, making mistakes in front of an audience hurts. I ran a Kickstarter which failed to reach its target. We planned a brilliant campaign, lined up support from friends and family, built an enthusiastic audience of early adopters, got press and PR coverage, but, despite a pitch-perfect launch, our donations flatlined after a few days. It was mortifying – our precious campaign had failed.

Rather than hiding from the world and wallowing in self-pity, I picked myself up, learnt from the experience and, in so doing, turned what was a failure into a new business opportunity. I realised the campaign was an experiment to test demand for a product. It was hugely valuable to find that out before we'd spent time and money building it. It might have failed, but it failed fast.

Some organisations see failure as the route to success. Take Google's sister company, X, where staff embrace failure. In fact, they are rewarded for it, with cash bonuses.

It might sound counterintuitive to hand out cash for failure; for most of us, our reward for a workplace mistake is a negative progress review, or a cardboard box to clear out our desks. But Astro Teller, who heads up X, explains that if you don't reward people for failing, 'they won't take risks and make breakthroughs. If you don't reward failure, people will hang on to a doomed idea for fear of consequences.' [60]

A failed idea saves time, money and resources, leaving remaining ideas to compete for survival. On its website, X states that thousands of its ideas last for a few hours, hundreds last for a few days, and dozens last for a few weeks or months.[61] Surviving ideas get stronger, and X joins forces with partners to make them real. One day, these ideas will change the lives of millions, if not billions, of people.

Teller tells his staff to be responsibly irresponsible, to 'explore, to take risks, to run experiments, to learn from those things and then repeat. And doing that really productively is uncomfortable.'

While it might be uncomfortable, it's part of the process. Think of it like the first time you tried to rollerblade, ice skate or ski – if you're not falling over, you're not learning.

Startup innovation expert Steve Blank says that successful founders 'go quickly from failure to failure, all the while adapting, iterating on, and improving their initial ideas as they continually learn from customers'.[62]

Blank is not recommending would-be entrepreneurs leave a trail of destruction and chaos; instead he's encouraging you to learn before you invest too much time, money and resources.

That idea was developed by Eric Ries into *The Lean Startup* – the go-to guide on starting a startup. In the book, he tears up the traditional business model approach to building a company and encourages entrepreneurs to focus on learning, rather than perfect paperwork.

The fundamental activity of a lean startup is to turn ideas into products. This is done by using a simple 'build–measure–learn' feedback loop. Entrepreneurs create ideas and build prototypes and MVPs, validate them by running frequent experiments with customers, and use that feedback to make decisions. Sometimes the learning leads to a pivot – a substantial change to the product, market or business model. We'll dig into pivots in the next chapter.

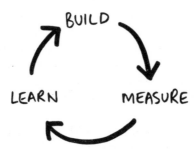

Founders cycle around the feedback loop, applying learning to rebuild and retest in the search for product/market fit and a scalable business model. The development process becomes about small incremental change, known in the lean movement as iteration. Iteration happens as quickly as possible.

Accept that you'll encounter some failures as you develop your idea. I'm not encouraging you to celebrate every small mistake, just to see failure as an opportunity to learn and improve. The hard knocks you receive as your idea develops will make you stronger and more resilient. Rather than developing a hard edge, grit has been linked to happiness.[63] Keep optimistic and frame your setbacks in positive language to increase your learning and give you hope to keep going.

Now's the time to use all the insight, feedback and data you gathered to reflect and make decisions. You might be forced to change course, or your learning could propel you in your current direction. Either way, as your idea gains momentum, you'll grow along with it.

FAILURE AS AN OPPORTUNITY TO LEARN

The first thing I noticed about Rob Fitzpatrick were his flip-flops. It was a typically cold, grey autumn day in Leeds with the threat of rain ever present. I assumed he had made a clothing fail, but this sun-charmed entrepreneur greets the English weather each day all year round by wearing flip-flops, most often paired with a brightly-coloured Hawaiian shirt. We should channel his attitude when the dark clouds gather.

Why, you might ask, should we take the advice of an underdressed American?

Fitzpatrick hit the startup jackpot by getting accepted into the Y Combinator technology accelerator in 2007. He summarises his first startup experience by saying: 'We didn't know what we were doing, and I ended up messing up a bunch of crucial sales meetings before we ultimately went out of business three years later.'

That happens to over 90 per cent of startups: they start, they struggle, they fail.[64] What separates founders who go on to do well is not their initial success, but their attitude. Fitzpatrick took time to learn from his dark moments, and eventually benefited from the painful experience. With a theory of what he'd done wrong, he applied his knowledge to new endeavours and got better results; since then he's been sharing the fruits of his failure with budding entrepreneurs through his writing and workshops.

Back in his early startup days, Fitzpatrick and his co-founders spent six months building a shiny new analytics dashboard, custom-designed to meet the needs of their most important client, one of the big media studios. It offered: 'a zillion options and could carve up your data every which way. It was technically and aesthetically lovely. Unfortunately, 90 per cent of what we had built was irrelevant.'[65]

He made a classic mistake of giving the client what they said they wanted without figuring out *why* they wanted it.

The client had asked for analytics, but if his team had properly understood why the client wanted analytics, he explains, 'we would have built a totally different (and much simpler) set of features. Consider how much easier our lives would have been if we'd understood the motivation behind the request.'

For an early-stage startup low on money, resource and time, this was an epic fail. It wasn't his only one.

It's one thing misunderstanding requests from your existing clients. It's far more dangerous failing to get clients in the first place. This was the mistake that Fitzpatrick made again and again. They had a great product, but people just weren't buying it.

Fitzpatrick knew he needed help. He sought out books on mastering the art of the deal, but they weren't making a difference; he was still messing up his sales meetings. He says:

'I was such a bad/inexperienced salesperson, I needed someone to show me *how* to talk to customers. The epiphany for how to do it happened when a mentor came with me to a key meeting. As soon as he saw what I was doing, he cut me off and took over the meeting, and having caught me in the act, he was able to give specific enough advice about what I was doing wrong and what I should be doing differently.'

Now that is tough – you're all pumped to win over a new client, and, mid-pitch, someone steps in and takes over, then afterwards gives you a lecture on all the stuff you're doing wrong.

But for Fitzpatrick it was an invaluable learning experience, one which required him to be humble enough to acknowledge and accept his mistakes and open enough to learn and improve.

LEARNING HOW TO LEARN

Opportunities to learn happen all the time – we just need to be able to spot them. One way to get better at noticing them is to regularly review what you've done.

Modern productivity gurus swear by self-reflection for boosting psychological well-being, but its origins lie in ancient Greece with the Stoic philosophers.

Stoics aspired to develop a clear, unbiased way of thinking – this meant rejecting emotion in favour of facts, as they put it, in accordance with nature. Rather than the po-faced pessimists they're often portrayed as, the Stoics believed that self-knowledge helped us to become better humans and live a good, or worthwhile, life.

Stoic thinker Epictetus said: 'From the first to the last, review your acts and then reprove yourself for wretched acts, but rejoice in those done well.'[66] Epictetus promoted a daily reckoning, ideally done at night, using three simple questions: 'Where did I go wrong? What did I do? And what duty's left undone?'

I used a version of these questions at the start of my career when I managed large digital projects. However, we only reviewed the project once it was completed, by which time it was too late to apply any learning. So much for iteration – it was better luck next time!

The point is to build regular reflection into how you work, so you're able to spot mistakes and quickly correct them. Yes, you know what I'm about to say: fail fast.

HOW TO REFLECT: ALONE AND WITH OTHERS

It only takes a few minutes to reflect. Start by answering these questions:

- What went well?

- What didn't go so well?

- What can I do better?

These questions are broad enough to apply throughout your idea journey – from reviewing brainstorms and prototyping sessions to pitches or tests of your MVP and sales techniques. It's as simple as making a few notes, celebrating the good stuff, noting what didn't work, and reflecting on how to adapt and change in the future. Don't dwell on your mistakes but accept them, learn and move on.

Get into the habit of doing this, maybe by keeping a daily journal where you reflect on how the day has gone. Or, you might reflect after specific activities – like sending an email, having a meeting, or writing a blog or advert. The key thing is to focus on the small happenings so you can adjust how you work without it being too big a deal.

A few minutes reflection can have a big impact – and fast. Researchers found that people who wrote or voice recorded about significant events – both positive and negative ones – reported improved life satisfaction and enhanced mental and physical health relative to those who only thought about them. This uptick was found after only three days of doing this exercise.[67]

Fitzpatrick was lucky to have a mentor who helped him reflect and learn. If you're working alone, seek out a mentor or group of advisors you can rely on to help you review and offer perspective on what you are doing – there's advice on this later in the book. It certainly helps when you have others to review with – and necessary if you're working on a group project. If you're part of a team, make the most of other people's viewpoints.

Build a moment for review at the end of co-working and it quickly becomes part of the way you collaborate. It builds trust, empathy and understanding across teams. It's easy to do, and shouldn't be a big deal.

Grab some Post-it notes and pens and find a quiet place to work together, ideally with a wall you can stick notes to. Work individually for a few minutes, answering the three questions from the opposite page by writing one reflection per Post-it note, and writing as many reflections as you need.

Label three Post-it notes: one with 'did well', the next with 'not so well', and the third with 'do better'. Even better just draw emojis: smiley face, sad face, and thinking face. Stick them on a wall first, leaving plenty of space between them.

Just like in a brainstorm, one person kicks off by sharing a reflection and sticking up their note. If someone else has a similar thought, they read theirs and stick it up alongside the first note. Together, you'll create clusters of similar reflections.

Once everything is on the wall, you'll quickly identify patterns. Use these to acknowledge mistakes, target areas for improvement, and agree actions based on what you've learnt.

It's most effective to focus on just one thing you can do and build that into your work immediately. You can even kick off the next session with it, so you have a plan to make it happen. No need to write up the notes, just take a photo, and share it on your messaging platform of choice.

REJOICE

As well as learning from things that don't go well, the Stoics urged their students to celebrate. Don't forget the second part of Epictetus' quote, 'rejoice in those [acts] done well'.

Taking time to celebrate is not only fun, it boosts resilience, reinforces well-being and creates a happiness-seeking mindset. You don't need to throw a party, just taking time to notice what went well makes a difference.

Research by the founder of positive psychology, Professor Martin Seligman, has shown that noticing good things each day, and expressing gratitude for them, can have a long-term impact on well-being.[68] Seligman, a psychologist at the University of Pennsylvania, tested the impact of various positive psychology interventions. In one study, he asked participants to write and personally deliver a letter of gratitude; they exhibited a huge increase in happiness scores, and, although only asked to do this for a week, the benefits lasted for a month. In another test, he got participants to write down three good things each day; the positive impact of this exercise was still measurable six months after they had stopped doing it.

One of the reasons these exercises have such long-lasting effects is that they condition you to notice good things throughout the day. You become a happiness-seeker.

If you're working with others, you can help your team towards greater positivity by designing celebration rituals. The simplest is just saying 'thank you' when things go well. Researchers found that managers who say thank you can boost their team's performance by an extra 50 per cent.[69] This 'prosocial behaviour' spreads the benefits of gratitude and makes others feel good. You can work rituals into any group activity by encouraging collaboration, highlighting good work or celebrating when projects come to an end.

Grab any opportunity you can to reflect and rejoice – together they will lead to compound growth. Read on to find out more.

DEVELOPING A GROWTH MINDSET

The benefits of reflection and rejoicing are clear: reflection allows you to spot opportunities for adjusting your behaviour to prevent making time-consuming, costly mistakes; celebrating small wins will keep you motivated on your hustle. But to make the most of this meta skill, you must learn how to learn. The goal is to cultivate a mindset that is open to learning from experimentation, failure and feedback.

Dr Carol S. Dweck has spent her career researching what makes people succeed. The Stanford University psychology professor found that to foster success people need a 'growth mindset', and that people who have this are more able to learn than those with a 'fixed mindset'.

Dweck says of those with a growth mindset: 'Not only are people with this mindset not discouraged by failure, but they don't actually see themselves as failing in those situations – they see themselves as learning.' (Remember how we talked about 'reframing' failure?)

Dweck's studies completely overturned the popular view that innate talent determines achievement. It's easy to look at famous entrepreneurs and think: they were born that way; they're the lucky ones with the money-making genes; and to think, by turn, that we aren't cut out to be entrepreneurs. But, when you dig a little deeper, you find 'the lucky ones' didn't learn how to make money, but how to cope when they didn't and still continue. And the good news is that we too can develop a similar mindset.

TRAINED TO FAIL, LEARN AND GROW

Every afternoon when Sara Blakely got back from school, her dad would ask: 'What have you failed at today?' [70]

Before you think someone should have called child services, Blakely's dad wasn't bullying her but building an attitude of trying. And Blakely is a trier. She launched Spanx, the multimillion-dollar company, without any knowledge of how to design, make and sell underwear. She made a lot of mistakes, and each error made her more persistent. When she got her first order, Blakely couldn't fulfil it because her product needed gussets, but she hadn't known what a gusset was, so hadn't made them. It was a race against time to find a supplier, manufacture the gussets, then insert them, so she could ship her fully-functional product.

From an early age Blakely, pushed herself beyond her 'natural abilities'. Her dedication and hard work created a resilience to bounce back from failure and enabled her to reach high levels of entrepreneurial success.

Success hasn't stopped Blakely making mistakes, but she relishes opportunities that would make most of us curl up and die of embarrassment. She once messed up a big interview with the BBC when she talked about women's 'fannies', not understanding that the UK meaning is very different to the US one.

Blakely clearly has a growth mindset, one her father fostered in her school days. As Dweck says, this approach: 'creates a love of learning and a resilience that is essential for great accomplishment. Virtually all great people have had these qualities.'[71] It enables them to thrive in the most challenging situations.

HOW TO BUILD A GROWTH MINDSET

You're already in a great position to develop a growth mindset. Making your ideas happen gives you plenty of opportunity to learn and grow. Here are some key action points for innovators, based on Dweck's research:

- Start by valuing effort before talent.

- Enjoy the process rather than focussing on the end result.

- Reward your actions rather than your achievements.

- Change your attitude: see failure as learning.

- View challenges as opportunities. Things will go wrong; make the most of it.

- Be open to feedback and criticism; try to see the value in even the most negative comments.

- Learn from other people: their mistakes can be particularly helpful.

- Take risks, try new things, experiment, learn.

- Be persistent, and cultivate grit and determination.

- Finally, take time to reflect.

To be a founder is to fail – the verb, to founder, literally means to fail miserably. There's no getting away from it – you will fail as you develop your idea. The trick is to reframe that failure as learning.

Just like famous inventor Thomas Edison did: 'I haven't failed. I've just found ten thousand ways that do not work.' Edison had to work through those 10,000 failures to reach success. To be inventive, you have to get comfortable with failure and keep going until you reach success.

Remember my Kickstarter? If my goal had just been about reaching the financial target, then I had clearly failed. Instead, having learning as a goal meant that I couldn't fail. Everything I did was evidence I could use to make a better decision.

CHAPTER SUMMARY

- **In short**: Failure is just another word for learning.

- **Start now**: Channel your inner Stoic by reflecting on how things are going.

- **Go expert**: Learn how to learn by developing a growth mindset.

- **Be happy**: Reflect, rejoice in what went well, and cultivate positivity in your team.

- **Next step**: Apply the lean principles of build–measure–learn as you work out whether to quit or pivot.

CHAPTER TEN

Pivot

Teddle was failing. Eighteen months after launching the marketplace for local services, co-founder Alex Depledge was exhausted, overweight from stress-related binge eating, and ready to give up the startup dream for the security of a regular job.

'Nothing was working,' says Depledge. 'It felt like I was pushing water uphill. I told my co-founders Tom and Jules: "Guys, I'm out. It's not working for me. I'm embarrassed; it's an utter failure."'

At Christmas 2012, the three of them sat down to figure out what was going on. They pulled off all the data from the website to get a better idea of what users were doing.

Depledge says: 'We discovered that 75 per cent of all the traffic to our site was people looking for a cleaner. And we found that highly amusing because we didn't have any cleaners on the site! The penny dropped – they can't find cleaners: that's the problem. So Hassle.com was born.'

The pivot from Teddle to Hassle.com led to massive user growth, a multimillion-pound funding round, and eventual acquisition; it also bagged an MBE for Depledge's services to the sharing economy. However, it wasn't an easy decision to make. The founding team had invested time, energy and love in the original platform – they had quit their jobs, learnt to code, and they even named it after one of their dogs, Ted.

But they couldn't argue with the data. Depledge and her co-founders had to separate their emotions from the facts. In doing so, they understood that they had to change course. So might you.

QUIT, PIVOT OR PERSEVERE?

It's decision time. You've taken time out to reflect and learn from the journey so far, and now you need to decide what comes next.

If everything is hunky dory – you're happy, your audience is happy, the idea's a winner – then pop open the prosecco. You're ready to take your hustle to the next level, and Chapter 11 will help you grow your audience.

If something isn't working, you might face a junction in your journey: quit or pivot?

These are two very different pathways. You can't decide which route to take by flipping a coin – you need bravery, resilience and, most importantly, evidence.

Evidence will make the decision easier, though don't underestimate how tough it can be, especially if things haven't worked out as you hoped.

Sometimes the best decision is to quit. You might have had a blast creating and building your concept, and decided that's enough. Some people enjoy the thrill of the creation stage, but the slog of getting it to market is too much. If that's you, take time to celebrate what you've achieved.

You might, like Depledge, know that it's not working, but need more information or to better analyse the existing information, before calling it quits. Now's the time to take a long hard look at the data and consider the options for pivoting.

In this chapter, you'll bounce back from failure, put your new-found resilience into practice and:

- Decide whether to quit, pivot or persevere.

- Learn how to quit well.

- Get to grips with the different ways to pivot.

- Build the passion and perseverance to grow.

QUITTING IS BRAVE

We need to talk about quitting. Stand up straight, hold your head up high and take a deep breath – we're braving a taboo.

You're in the pits; it couldn't get any worse. If this were a film you'd be at the end of Act Two, stuck up a tree, naked and shoeless, with someone throwing rocks at you. You have no idea how to get down and find your happy ending.

Sometimes your happy ending involves quitting. And that is OK.

We're hardwired to stick with things, even when they don't work. If you've given your all to an idea, it's tough to let go. Economists call this a sunk cost: basically, investing time, money and passion in a project affects your judgement, and you start to justify your ongoing investment. This leads to something called the 'sunk cost fallacy' where that justification doesn't stack up: the costs of the decision to continue outweigh the expected benefit.

The textbook example of sunk cost fallacy is the United States' continued commitment to military conflict in Vietnam in the 1970s. A more recent business example is the Segway, which cost over $100 million in research and development costs, but failed to reach its annual sales target of half a million units a year – selling barely 30,000 total in the first six years.[72]

Having an idea for a side hustle is in no way like fighting a war (maybe it's a bit like riding a Segway, continuing to lean forwards even when you're on a dead-end path), but you get what I mean. You've put so much into it that it feels impossible to abandon, and the best option seems like continuing along your agreed plan of action – even when the most sensible option is to quit.

You just need to have the guts to do it.

KNOWING WHEN TO QUIT

Jo Caley was on a mission to end vanity sizing. Her website High Street Fit Finder was created to help women find jeans they loved, that fit them and made them feel good about themselves.

Caley developed and grew the website so that it was attracting customers, pulling in income and generating great PR. But website traffic had plateaued – although users were joining at a regular rate, it wasn't getting the week-on-week growth that's expected of tech startups. Caley tried everything to get traction: blogging, advertising, Facebook and Twitter, but, despite her best efforts, she couldn't move the needle.

The pressure was piling on to improve the figures and get investment to grow. Caley spent hours pitching, which left little time for her to update the website and manage the business. She says:

> 'The more I had to put myself out there and pitch for funding, [the more] I was beginning to feel really uncomfortable. I was having to concentrate on figures and spreadsheets and business plans, and, while I enjoyed learning how to do those things, doing them and presenting them and talking about them I really hated.'

Caley questioned why she was doing it. She was neglecting the parts of the business she most enjoyed, spending time doing activities she didn't like, and she had started to feel anxious about her ability to grow the business as a sole founder. In short, she had fallen out of love with her idea.

After four years of incredibly hard work, and countless hours teaching herself how to build a business, she stopped. The website and all the social channels remained live, but she no longer updated or promoted them.

For a while she felt guilty, thinking of all the time and investment, but as the months passed, her attention turned elsewhere. She got a new job and bought a house with her partner. They got a puppy. She had a life and time to call her own. As she reached the fifth anniversary of her idea, she took the website down.

The sizing problem is a tough one to crack; many people around the world have tried, but none have succeeded. Caley gave High Street Fit Finder everything she could. She might not have solved the problem, but trying to build a solution gave her a whole new set of skills and experiences that have changed her life for the better. She says:

> 'I wouldn't have been able to get my job had I not done the work on High Street Fit Finder, and I wouldn't have been paid the money I got paid if I didn't have the skills that I had learnt doing those things. I learnt how to code; I learnt how to analyse data; I learnt how to build websites; I learnt a lot about starting up a business and all the effort it takes and how things do not happen overnight. I met some lovely people. I met some not very nice people. But I learnt how to deal with those not very nice people.'

Despite all the stress, the hard work and dealing with the not very nice people, Caley is proud of her work, what she learnt, and the effort it took to build her idea. She might not have been able to scale it, but it solved a problem for many women.

'I'm pleased I did it,' she says. 'It was a good idea. If I hadn't done it, I would have wondered: "What if?"'

Caley ticks all the boxes for having a growth mindset – she extracted all the learning she could from solving her problem, and has much to celebrate.

HOW TO QUIT WELL

It's hard admitting that something hasn't worked out as you planned, but there are ways of holding your head high when things go wrong. Try this four-step approach to quitting well.

1. **Decide**. Make your decision to quit based on evidence. This keeps the emotion out of it and will reduce feelings of blame and guilt.

2. **Celebrate**. Review what worked, as well as what didn't, and then reward yourself for your effort and successes – you earned it.

3. **Learn**. Think about what you could do differently or better next time. Find those learning opportunities, and use them as the foundation for future plans.

4. **Plan**. Make a plan for your next move. You've learnt so much from your hustle, and, although it might not feel like it, you're a wiser, stronger person with new skills and experiences to put into practice.

While your first instinct might be to hit the pub to drown your sorrows (to be honest, that sometimes works, especially if you go with good mates), there are lots of other healthy and more psychologically boosting things to do.

Get social

Being around people who like, love and support you will give you perspective. There's a reason the most grounded celebrities have the same bunch of friends they had pre-fame. Rather than an entourage desperate for sprinkles of stardust, old friends and family have weathered all the ups and downs, and still like the person who went through it all.

Exercise

Deep breathing, meditation and yoga all counter stress; however, these are a long-term practice and not just a 'break in emergency' solution. While I meditate daily and channel my inner yogi with Ashtanga yoga each week, when things go wrong I let rip by boxing. Hitting a punch bag hard is extremely cathartic. While high intensity exercise is proven to be most effective in reducing stress, any form of exercise, including walking and hiking helps.[73] And, as a bonus, it boosts creativity – you might find that before you've put one idea to bed, another one springs to life.

Review

Reviewing how things went provides closure. We're so used to feeling we should always do more, better, but it's important to celebrate what went well. Rather than looking at your mountain of a to-do list, write a 'done' list. Feel that dopamine hit when you tick off all the things you've accomplished. Or go one step further and write a 'ta-da' list of the truly brilliant things you've achieved.

Reward

You've now got a long list of things to reward yourself for. What's on your done list? What are you most proud of on your ta-da list? What things did you do you that you thought you'd never do? Go celebrate – you deserve it. If you worked with others, include them in the celebrations. Or you might prefer to send them a thank you – we spoke about the psychological benefits of gratitude in Chapter 9. So, hit messenger and send some appreciation, or go old-school and pen them a postcard.

Time travel

Another tip is to time travel and imagine what your past self would think of how far you've come. Since I first held books in my jam-covered toddler hands, I have dreamt of writing one. My three-year-old self would be stoked I'm writing this – hell, my 33-year-old self would be even more excited.

Write

It's a bit of a cliché to write your quit story, but there's a reason so many startup founders head to Medium to post their musings. Writing has been shown to reduce PTSD, anxiety and depression;[74] it helps you think through what happened. It doesn't need to be public – most of the research was based on getting people to write a private journal. Channel your inner Adrian Mole.

Update your skills

You've got a list of things you learnt and can do better – it might feel too soon to write a business plan for your next venture, so you could take a small step by updating your LinkedIn profile with your kickass new skills. You could get a few recommendations from co-collaborators or people you tested ideas with.

If things haven't gone as planned, take a break and give yourself time to work through it. Acknowledging what went wrong is the first step in getting closure and moving ahead.

THE HARD THING ABOUT STARTUPS

Vix Anderton describes her introduction to the startup way as a 'crash course'. All around her people were burning out. She remembers how founders would share their stories. 'They were all talking about how hard it was,' Anderton says, 'and even then I was like: "That sounds horrible. I don't want to do hard."'

Anderton is not afraid of hard things. An ex-RAF intelligence officer, she spent ten years working in some of the most dangerous places in the world and is an expert in assessing risk in conflict zones. So, what was it about startups?

'We live in a culture now,' she says, 'that glorifies work and hustle and achievements, and always being on the go – this whole you'll sleep when you're dead thing.'

She saw what was going on around her, what people were putting themselves through to achieve their dreams, and she refused to subscribe to it.

Anderton had experienced depression herself, when overwork had driven her to have suicidal thoughts. It was scary and lonely and dark, and there was no way she was going back. Her life was good; she was having an amazing summer and was feeling happy and healthy. Under no circumstances would she compromise that.

That became the problem she set out to solve. Anderton knew that to work well, you have to rest well, so she set up The Practical Balance to help founders reset their lives. This involves finding purpose and meaning in work, while also taking time to rest, relax and enjoy life.

You need to start with the basics, advises Anderton: looking at your well-being and healthy habits, getting enough sleep and taking breaks to recharge and keep perspective. Her work, informed by her experience in the military, involves changing people's mindset. Take the idea of a debrief – Anderton explains:

> 'The military, especially the Royal Air Force is really big on debriefing. Every time an aircrew goes flying, there's a clear mission brief before they go, so they are really clear on what it is they're doing, what they want to get out of it. And then they have a debrief when they get back. One of the things for me is encouraging people to know themselves, to make time for reflection: what went well today, what didn't go well today, what do I want to build on tomorrow?'

As we saw in the last chapter, reflection will help you grow – but only if you put your learning into practice. To bounce back from failure, you need to try again.

NEXT! START AGAIN

Richard Branson is famed for his multiple Virgin-branded ventures which comprise a business portfolio worth billions. He also has a whole heap of failed enterprises. Take Virgin Brides, Cola, Digital, Clothing, Games – these and so many others were set up and shut down.

But no one would call Branson a quitter – he's a superhero for wannabe tycoons. Branson believes that people don't notice failed ideas and is inspo-quoted all over the internet for saying: 'If your idea doesn't work, not many people will have noticed. Keep pushing on to the next idea.'

When something goes wrong, he has already moved on and is busy making plans for what's next, seeking another gap in the market, hunting a new opportunity.[75] While we might not have Branson's business balls, we can emulate his courage by focussing on what's next.

Playwright Samuel Becket wrote: 'Ever tried. Ever failed. No matter. Try Again. Fail again. Fail better.'[76] In the last chapter, we learnt why failure was a necessary part of the creation process. It will be painful and embarrassing but by reframing failure as learning, you build resilience. That helps you fail better.

'Fail better' is more than a neat soundbite. Like the feedback loop in the Lean Startup methodology, failing better is a process of repetition and iteration. That's why it's so important to make failures small, quick and early in the life of your idea – it makes it easier to bounce back. If you want to level up your idea, you need to try again and master the art of the pivot.

THREE PIVOTS: PROBLEM, SOLUTION, PEOPLE

If something's not quite right, but quitting isn't on the cards, then you need to pivot.

A pivot is a substantial change to your idea, and it's not something to be taken lightly. It doesn't mean you're starting from scratch, but rather that you're running a new experiment to see if it gets better results than the previous one.

Some of the most successful startups are the result of pivots – take Slack, the fastest growing startup ever, anywhere in the world. We know it now as a team communication tool, but it began as an internal system for developers working on an online game called Glitch. The game failed, but the messaging system took off, and the company behind it raised an eye-watering $120 million of investment for its 'Searchable Log of All Conversation and Knowledge'.

Pivots take time and effort, so make sure your decisions about what to do next are evidence-based. The first thing to is decide what sort of a pivot you're taking. There are three types:

Problem pivot

You're solving the wrong problem. As you share your idea with people, you realise there's a bigger, better or more exciting problem for you to solve.

Solution pivot

You've got the right problem, but the solution isn't right. You need an alternative solution, or one based on just one element of your solution. For example, people have the problem, but they only need one part of your concept or a particular feature.

People pivot

You've got the right problem and a great solution, but the wrong market. As you listen to users, you find there's a segment of your audience that loves your idea, so focus on them instead. Perhaps you'd designed something for women aged 25–45, but only those over 40 got really excited about it.

Let's take each pivot in turn.

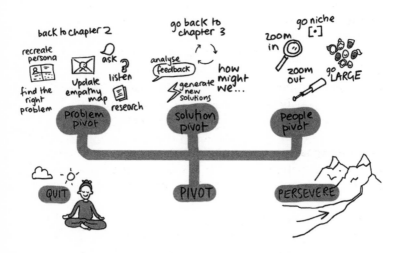

PROBLEM PIVOT

At the top of the chapter we met Teddle, the marketplace for local services that pivoted to become Hassle.com, the place to find cleaners. Alex Depledge told us how the founding team looked at the data and figured out they were solving the wrong problem.

But what was the original problem they were trying to solve?

Meet Depledge's co-founder, Jules Coleman, who back in 2011 had plans to brush up her piano practice. She was looking online for a local teacher, and the search results sucked: she could find piano teachers, but there wasn't enough information or any ratings or recommendations to indicate quality.

Many startups grow from a problem one of the founders has, and Coleman figured if she needed a piano teacher, so must other people. She was right, but why stop at piano? What about other types of teachers, trainers and services? The problem snowballed to contain search and matching for 27 types of local service providers, from driving instructors to dog walkers. Many services, but not the one service most people needed – as Depledge explained, three-quarters of visitors to the website were searching for cleaners. That was the problem to solve.

The solution was already created, so the team dug into this new problem and pivoted their existing business to better meet the needs of people looking for cleaners and the needs of cleaners looking for safe jobs and a regular income.

If you have the wrong problem but the right solution, you're in a great place to pivot. You've already developed and tested your concept, so you've got all the skills and experience to move forward and, you've got a solution to build on.

Immerse yourself in the new problem. This time you have people to help you, so let them. Start with their feedback to understand how they frame the problem. You might need to do more research. Go out and talk to people who experience this new problem; perhaps recreate your personas and empathy maps (see Chapter 2). Get their problem front of mind as you move ahead.

SOLUTION PIVOT

If the feedback shows the solution just isn't working, don't chuck the whole thing in the bin – you've got options.

Go back to your feedback from users and take a closer look at the comments. You might have concluded that the current iteration isn't working – set that result to one side and dive into what they liked. What were they interested in? What expectations did they have? Which features did they want to try? Even better, find the love in any positive reactions and follow that.

In Chapter 6, we looked at evaluating feedback – it's worth redoing this exercise, digging through to find patterns in people's wants and needs. Verbatim feedback is excellent, but can you remember the tone with which someone made a comment, or how they reacted? A positive response is displayed in more than words, so look for what triggered their attention or excitement.

You might find that people don't want the whole solution but love a single element. Home in on this to figure out what interested them and why. In this case, you don't need to build anything new; instead go out and test what's already there, asking people just about that one element of the solution.

If you've dug through all the research and failed to find a single positive comment or reaction, then you still have opportunities. From talking to people, you know the problem exists, but you just haven't created the right solution.

Go back to the original problem, write another 'How might we …' statement, and brainstorm new ideas. You're not starting from scratch – you've got a brilliant first idea to riff off, so go wild, channel your users' needs, and create something that will wow them. Revisit Chapter 3 for tips. Then retest it in the smallest, quickest possible way, perhaps even speaking to some of the people you originally tested with.

Solution pivots are a classic Lean Startup iteration, building on what you've done to make your idea stronger.

In Chapter 7 we saw how Anne-Marie Imafidon took an experimental approach to iterate Stemettes. Over the years Imafidon and her team created what they call The Stemette Way, their guiding mission and values, which included the events being: 'free for the girls, fun for the girls, and there being food. And even then,' says Imafidon, 'we're still iterating because music is also a big part of what we do.'

It takes time to hone a solution until it works – sometimes it's a small iteration, other times it's a more radical pivot. Through running experiments, observing what happens and working with feedback Stemettes ensures that its solution continues to work for its core audience.

THE PEOPLE PIVOT – ZOOM IN

A people pivot happens when you have the right problem and your solution is spot on, but you have the wrong market. There are two ways to fix this: you can zoom in or zoom out on users.

We used to describe Prolifiko as a digital writing coach for anyone who wants to write. Anyone? Yes! Anyone and everyone who wants to write.

Looking at the early data, that was right: the first users were all sorts of writers, from poets and playwrights, to novelists and non-fiction writers. We had data to prove it – I hand coded the first 1,000 users to categorise the type of writing they did. It took me all day, and it was fascinating to a writing geek like me, but it didn't tell me very much.

To find out who *really* had the problem, and which type of writer *actually* needed the solution we offered, we had to talk to people. Conversations with our early users gave us a depth of understanding that percentages never could. It helped us zoom in to one group of writers who suffered the problem more acutely than any other: academics and scholarly writers.

When we talked to academics, we found that mounting workloads, growing admin and management responsibilities make it increasingly hard for them to do the one thing that will advance their careers: write and publish research in top-tier journals.

Academics don't just want to write, they need to do it – their careers, salaries and reputations are dependent on their writing and research productivity.

Not only that, universities are now increasingly ranked (and therefore financed) on how prolific and prestigious their academic staff are – the 'publish or perish' pressure is intense. Understanding that was a breakthrough for us.

However, academics were one of the smaller proportions of our product users. If we had stuck to analysing 'big data', we'd have completely missed them and not understood their specific problem. Zooming in transformed our empathy, and we pivoted to focus on this group of users.

If you find you've got a different target market, get to know and understand them, talk to them and gather information about their lives. Use Chapter 2 to update your personas and empathy maps with new feedback.

Embrace your niche. Don't worry that it's a smaller market; if they love your idea they'll be more likely to buy it. That is exactly what happened with academics. After doing a series of interviews and updating our personas, we could tailor messages specifically to them. We designed a landing page to test this out, and found in a few weeks that it converted 44.5 per cent of people visiting the site to leads who gave us their email address – that's over five times better than our generic landing page for writers.

This had an impact on our bottom line, because, by attracting academic writers more effectively, we lowered the cost of acquisition. It cost us less to acquire an academic user than to attract other writers.

Zooming in helped us find a set of writers who had suffered the problem more acutely than others, who were more passionate about our solution, and who were more likely to sign up to use it. The added bonus was that they cost less to find.

THE PEOPLE PIVOT - ZOOM OUT

John Kershaw had an idea. He was playing the startup idea generator game where you insert the name of a bigtime startup and combine it with another industry. He landed on 'Uber for beard fondling'. He explains the premise: 'I want to fondle a beard; I don't have a beard; click a button on an app, and off you go.'

It tickled him, so he decided to share the joke.

'That evening I came up with the name, Bristlr. I posted this to Facebook and lots of people were like, "Ah that's hilarious." So, I made a fake landing page with a Mailchimp sign-up form so that people could actually sign up to something. I started sharing it round on Facebook and Reddit and all these other communities, and I decided that if I could get 100 sign-ups, I would build a website.'

Kershaw hit his target and spent the next two weeks building a prototype. Because it's a funny idea that made people laugh and share it with their friends, it went viral and then got picked up by mainstream newspapers like the *Daily Mail*. Before long, he had 60,000 registered users for his prototype. While he admits his first version 'kind of sucked for a while', it was the perfect test of the concept and gave him the confidence to quit his job and seek investment to make it better.

With investment came brilliant advice and the realisation that the existing business model didn't work. Kershaw tried looking at different options for his core audience of beard lovers, exploring beard hair products and the like, but nothing quite worked. He had hit beard ceiling.

'It was never going to be a big business,' Kershaw says. 'Bristlr was profitable, but it wasn't scalable.'

Bristlr was a niche dating app for people who have beards and people who love to stroke beards. It was solving a problem for people, but in a limited market. Kershaw knew it worked – he had the wedding invites – but it wasn't going to grow.

Kershaw had the right problem and the right solution; it was the audience that was wrong. Niche dating isn't unique to beard lovers, so he zoomed out of his niche audience to pivot.

'Learning that Bristlr isn't scalable made us realise that if we increase the number of Bristlrs that we have, suddenly you hit exponential growth.'

Kershaw created M14 Industries to develop apps for clients to connect people in other 'niche' communities, from people seeking long-term relationships rather than Tinder hook-ups, to black professionals looking to grow their work network. Within six months, M14 Industries won a UK Dating Award and pitch competition Northern Stars, and when he entered the BBC's *Dragons' Den,* he got offers from all five investors. The pivot worked, and Kershaw was finally able to grow his business.

BUILD PASSION AND PERSEVERANCE TO GROW

Don't worry if the evidence suggests you need to pivot – nothing you've done so far is wasted. You've learnt a huge amount about your users, your solution and yourself. It's all part of the journey to making your idea happen.

Once you make it past the quit-or-pivot fork in the road, you'll soon be on the path to success – with this idea or the next one. It takes tenacity to keep going, as researcher Angela Duckworth says:

'Grit grows as we figure out our life philosophy, learn to dust ourselves off after rejection and disappointment, and learn to tell the difference between low-level goals that should be abandoned quickly and higher-level goals that demand more tenacity. The maturation story is that we develop the capacity for long-term passion and perseverance as we get older.'[77]

She's right: getting through this stage will increase your passion and commitment to your idea. By figuring out what path to take, you've developed the perseverance and wisdom to continue your hustle and grow your audience.

CHAPTER SUMMARY

- **In short**: It takes bravery to quit and time to figure out a pivot.

- **Start now**: Use evidence to decide whether to quit, pivot or persevere.

- **Go expert**: Breathe, meditate, walk, run, fight – use exercise to counter stress.

- **Be happy**: Enjoy the sense of satisfaction when the puzzle of the pivot clicks into place.

- **Next step**: Persevere – it's time to grow.

CHAPTER ELEVEN

Grow

'Holy shit.' Howard Kingston looked at the download figures for the football gaming app *I Am Playr*. He was head of marketing for the launch team. He had targets to meet, targets that were being revised each week.

When *I Am Playr* launched it quickly gained an impressive 50,000 users, but that soon dropped to 30,000 users and flatlined for months. The team worked frantically on fortnightly sprints, running experiment after experiment to test ideas attempting to gain new users.

The holy shit moment came six months in: they were growing by 80,000 users a day. *I Am Playr* smashed through target after target, and within eighteen months had 20 million users.

THE HOCKEY STICK OF SUCCESS

I Am Playr's growth curve resembled a hockey stick – it's the shape of success, what every early-stage startup seeks. But it's elusive. Even Kingston, a serial entrepreneur, didn't know how to get that kind of growth, and when he did, it blew his mind.

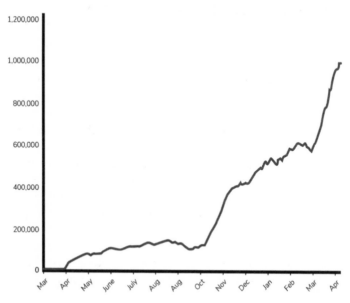

© Escape Velocity, reprinted with permission from Howard Kingston

'I would never have thought making a couple of tweaks could make something explode globally,' says Kingston. 'And they were small tweaks. If we had not done that one experiment, that one time, and brought that feature into the product, it would've been very different.'

The feature that caused exponential growth was a viral share: rewarding existing users for sharing *I Am Playr* with five friends. It meant that not only did Kingston's team smash their growth targets, they did so at no cost to the company. Existing users recruited new users – effectively doing the marketing for free.

This is a classic growth hacking tactic. Hacking is not a shortcut – Kingston and his team worked for months testing and experimenting until something worked. But when it worked, the result spoke for itself.

WHEN CUSTOMERS COME KNOCKING

Nineteenth-century philosopher and poet Ralph Waldo Emerson is often quoted by startup growth experts: 'If man has good corn, or wood, or boards, or pigs to sell, or can make better chairs or knives, crucibles, or church organs, than anybody else, you will find a broad, hard-beaten road to his house, though it be in the woods.'[78]

Nowadays mud tracks through the woods are more likely to be digital highways, but Emerson shares an eternal truth: if you build something that people want, they will come knocking – in droves. This chapter looks at what you can do to help your idea grow.

It's time to switch from product building to audience building. You're going to keep on testing and experimenting as you grow a community of early users.

Your idea might feel like a hot mess right now, but if people love it, then you're in the right place. Set aside your blushes, hold your nerve and resist the urge to 'finish'. Get ready to:

- Forget about perfection and the notion of a finished idea.

- Find product/market fit and cross the chasm to growth.

- Figure out how big your audience needs to be.

- Measure how much your users love your idea, with metrics.

FORGET FINISHING

Every time my Mum asks: 'Is your website finished yet?' I revert to my teenage self, avert my gaze and make excuses – it's never finished.

Throughout our lives, we're taught to complete things: do your homework and hand it in; run that 10K and pick up your medal; bake a cake and eat it. But an idea is a work in progress. In permanent beta, it is always improving and iterating as we optimise and learn.

It's hard to live in this never-quite-done state, with an open list of things to do preying on your mind – under your mother's compassionate gaze. Yet, it's liberating to no longer aim for perfection. Forget about a one-time launch. Free yourself from the goal of completion. Rather than aim for finish, focus on finding your fit.

All the work you've done so far shows you've solved a problem that matters and there's a demand for it. Hurrah! You've designed something that people want.

Now, are there enough people to make it a viable business? Do you have a market?

This stage is called product/market fit, and it's the pre-condition for growth.[79] It's described by San Francisco super-VC Marc Andreessen as 'being in a good market with a product that can satisfy that market'.

Satisfying the market is what gives you 'growth': increasing the number of people who engage with your idea (ideally by paying for it). In the earlier days of your hustle, you spent time understanding people, talking to them and getting feedback. You now need to take a step from engaging with a few passionate people to reaching a market of many. To achieve this, you need to 'cross the chasm'.

Pull on your hiking gear, we're heading to the mountains.

CONSIDERING THE CHASM

Finding and building an audience can feel like an uphill struggle, and just when you've climbed up a steep slope, you hit a precipice. Beyond it lie sunny uplands, but first you need to find a route across this divide. Geoffrey A. Moore in his classic book, *Crossing the Chasm*, took the typical technology adoption cycle – a bell curve of when groups of your market start using your product or service – and broke it up with small gaps between each group to show the extra effort required in reaching the next, bigger market.

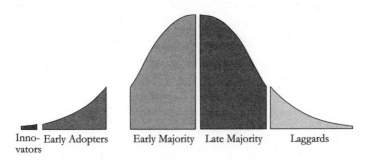

Inno- Early Adopters   Early Majority   Late Majority   Laggards
vators

Used by permission from Geoffrey A. Moore's *Crossing the Chasm*, 3rd Edition © 1991, 1999, 2002, 2014 by Geoffrey A. Moore

Moore also placed a daunting divide between early adopters and the early majority – this is the chasm you need to cross. On the other side is product/market fit, growth, scale, investment and perhaps a multimillion-dollar buy-out and a future sunning yourself in the

Caribbean. But first, you need to consider the chasm. Over to Moore to explain:

> 'Every truly innovative high-tech product starts out as a fad, something with no known market value or purpose but with "great properties" that generate a lot of enthusiasm within an "in crowd" of early adopters. That's the early market. Then comes a period during which the rest of the world watches to see if anything can be made of this; that is the chasm. If in fact something does come out of it ... then a new mainstream market segment follows, typically with a rapidity that allows its initial leaders to become very, very successful.'[80]

It's not just tech that follows this adoption cycle. It applies to all products and services: it's the way fashion spreads, starting with the in-crowd, heading to the high street on its way to passé. And it has always happened – our age of viral growth is the latest in a long history of adoption. Consider how quickly dance crazes can dominate world dancefloors, from the Charleston to the Mashed Potato to the moonwalk to twerking.

Twerking started in the 1980s New Orleans bounce music scene. Its innovators were rappers and DJs hosting block parties in African-American communities. By the 1990s it spread to early adopters in hip-hop and rap culture, going beyond New Orleans to the wider American south including Miami, Memphis and Houston.

By the early 2000s it was namechecked by the rap community and featured in rap and R&B music videos. Its status with the early majority was assured when Beyoncé referenced it.

Twerking spread beyond the black community and went viral when popstar Miley Cyrus incorporated it into her routines. When she performed on MTV's Video Music Awards in August 2013, it became the top 'What is' Google search of the year and was firmly established in the late majority.

It was downhill from there to the laggards. I'm looking at you Taylor Swift.

Twerking was a mainstream phenomenon, featured on TV shows like *Glee*, discussed on chat shows and debated in regard to cultural appropriation. It got a reputation for being highly sexualised – a world away from its origins when men and women twerked equally on the dance floor. It hit rock bottom when Norwegian striker Ada Hegerberg was asked to twerk when she accepted the prestigious Ballon d'Or award for footballing prowess in 2018.

Growth is not a sure thing. Only a few get to be fashionable. Let's get to grips with the challenges of the chasm.

FIND YOUR BEACHHEAD

In a traditional business process, if you've got an amazing new idea, your boss will ask you to write up a business plan. One of the most important sections of such a plan concerns market size. That's where many people hit the buffers. When you start considering a huge market, and the way you are going to reach it, you get overwhelmed with the size of the task ahead and the impossibility of conquering it.

Facing a market growth chasm can stimulate your fight or flight response, in exactly the same way as it might when you face a crevasse in mountaineering. The way to overcome that fear is by breaking the task ahead into small manageable steps. Rather than spending time sizing the market opportunity, we're going to start with where you are now, with a handful of people who like your idea: these are the innovators – the beginning of the adoption cycle – by working with them you can cross the divide.

Don't look ahead to the crevasse and risk toppling in; instead, focus on where you are now and keep a firm footing as you move one step at a time.

How many people have you spoken to about your idea? How many people have tested it, use it regularly, and have paid? Perhaps five or ten, maybe 50?

While we might dream of immediate viral growth, the reality for most people is they have a small audience who have engaged with their idea. This handful of people is all you need to grow; marketing types call this a 'beachhead', named after the military manoeuvre when an attacking army takes control of an area of land near the sea before advancing further.

Startup bros love a war metaphor, and beachhead marketing with its overtures of do-or-die makes you feel proud to fight for your idea's survival. You advance into enemy territory, attack your opponents and competitors, and gain ground by taking customers from them in battle after battle.

I don't know about you, but when I was getting started with my side hustle, I didn't have enough energy to launch an assault. I had a job, a life, a bunch of commitments – I was tired, confused and trying to figure out what to do. I needed encouragement to keep going, not a call to arms.

What kept me going was love not war.

Take the first few people who tried our MVP. Their valuable feedback motivated me to continue, encouraged me to do more and better for them, and to find more people like them. We gained ground through understanding and empathy.

Nor did I have time to battle our competitors. Instead, by working with people in the same space, we became friends rather than enemies, and built alliances not opposing armies.

Don't focus on the majority you hope to reach. Get to know your existing users better, and engage with your competitors.

Jon Bradford confirms this approach, from his experience running accelerators and working with thousands of startups across Europe. He tells me: 'Founders who create solutions and products in a vacuum are very likely to fail, engaging with their customers too late and leaving too little time to course-correct.' Bradford advises:

'You can never speak to your prospective customer too much and too early. The best founders are those obsessed with their customers – always speaking to and learning from them – to understand how to better address their wants and needs.'

By getting to know your early users – even just a handful of them – you figure out their needs and wants. More importantly, you form relationships, spot connections between people and build not just an audience but a community.

While the eventual goal will be to get them (and others) to love your idea, start by tapping into the things they love now. If you're lucky, you might already love these things yourself.

HOW BIG IS BIG ENOUGH?

'How big could this get?' is the classic question investors ask to size up your ambition and potential for scale. It's a fair question but one I hate being asked; I hate the binary choice between a business being venture capital-backed or a 'lifestyle business' – the latter being clearly the wrong answer. Investors want to hear you say you have a billion-dollar unicorn so that they can 10X their investments. We'll talk about financing options and their pros and cons in the next chapter, but for now, let's consider: how big is big enough?

Answering this will help you figure out the path your idea will take. It will determine how you spend your time, the tasks you do and the satisfaction you'll feel as your hustle aligns with your answer. There is no right answer – only you know your underlying motivations and ambitions. Before you decide your route, let's hear the argument for small.

'Instead of trying to reach the large undifferentiated masses, seek the smallest viable audience,' advises marketing guru and modern-day business philosopher Seth Godin. He knows what he's talking about. Godin has spoken and written about building 'tribes' for many years. A tribe is a social unit based on shared values and ideas, and by forming and being a part of a tribe, you can make big changes.[81]

Let's get back to small. Godin says that the smallest viable audience does several things:

> 'First of all, it requires you to make better work, because if there's only 500 people in the core group you are serving – you better delight them and you better blow them away, because otherwise they won't tell their friends. Number two, it is truly achievable, because if you can describe the 500 people you seek to serve, you can find them and you can afford to reach them.' [82]

If you aim to grow to 500 people or a thousand the steps required are smaller and more manageable.[83] Forget about needing millions of dollars or millions of customers – instead build a passionate following.

A FAMILY OF FANS

'Shared passion,' says founder and community builder Wil Benton, 'is a very important underpinning of building a community, because if you haven't got a shared passion, you're not going to build a community.'

Benton's passion for music led him from blogging about his clubbing experience to sharing DJ mixes online, launching a record label, FatKidOnFire, growing a community of over 100,000 electronic music fans, and co-founding Chew, a live streaming platform for music that was acquired after scaling to 400,000 users in 190 countries. What, I asked, got him started?

'Bagpipes' was not the answer I expected to hear.

'It's a very impressive instrument,' Benton says. 'It's an instrument of war, designed for communicating between clans in valleys, so it makes a fuck load of noise, but if you're well skilled, it sounds incredible.'

Benton's family moved to Scotland when he was seven, and what started as a bit of a joke became a way for him to fit into a new school environment. He learnt to play the bagpipes, joined a regional pipe band and played throughout his teenage years. He stopped playing when he went to university in London. Instead there was a burgeoning dubstep and grime club scene that formed his new clan.

He became a regular in the basement clubs of East London. 'I'd start meeting the DJs and the producers that would play there,' Benton says. 'You go enough times and meet enough people, you start building relationships with the artists that are performing. Then they introduce you to people that they work with and it snowballs from there.'

Many of us can trace passions back to childhood hobbies like writing, drawing, dancing and generally having fun. So it was for Benton. 'Growing up,' he says, 'live music was a very important part of how we spent time together as a family.' His parents were fans, and regularly took Benton and his brother to see live music, from the guitar greats like Eric Clapton and Dave Gilmore to classical concerts. Music was how his parents relaxed, spent time with friends and met new people.

Building relationships lies at the core of how Benton built a community.

A FEW PASSIONATE ENTHUSIASTS

'People tend to think of communities as huge groups of people,' Sarah Drinkwater says, 'but two or three passionate enthusiasts are so much more contagious.'

As a vintage clothes and music fan, Drinkwater felt very alone growing up in a small village in the 1990s. Then along came the world wide web. 'The early days of the internet,' she says, 'were revolutionary for me in terms of finding people who didn't make me feel so alone: they became my tribe.'

When she moved to London she found a new tribe – both online and offline. She had a blog about London and organised meetups to bring people together. By connecting with like-minded people, Drinkwater uncovered the power of community, and became one of the UK's most prominent online community builders. This rare skill caught the attention of Google in the late noughties, and Drinkwater was hired to build startup communities, first with Google Maps then Google Campus.

What started as a need for connection became a set of skills and a passion that Drinkwater shares with the world. Her tried and tested advice for building a community is to begin with these three simple questions:

1. What do you deeply care about?

2. Who else cares about it?

3. How could you find them?

So, how would Benton answer Drinkwater's questions?

1. He cares deeply about live music.

2. This passion was initially shared by his family, then by friends at school, university and finally by fellow clubbers, DJs and promoters.

3. They could be found in small venues in East London and then online, which is where Benton's snowball gathers momentum.

'It was my first real taste of the power of sharing a passion on the internet with people that could relate to that passion,' Benton says of the experience of documenting the club nights on a blog, then posting DJ mixes on SoundCloud. SoundCloud was the place for people who liked a relatively obscure kind of electronic music. The platform made it easy to find and share cool tracks, which DJs would play at their next gigs.

'When I first uploaded long-form content in the form of DJ mixes, they were lucky to get ten to 50 plays.' Benton's first followers were friends and family. But through blogging and posting mixes consistently, he met more DJs and producers, and grew an online community of fans.

'I remember being amazed the first time a mix went past 1,000 plays. It was start from zero and build an archive of content.' By 2014 he was uploading three to five posts and two mixes a day to an audience on SoundCloud of 50,000 followers; combined with his followers on platforms like Mixcloud and Facebook, he was reaching over 100,000 people globally.

That's quite a community, grown from a family love of music.

COMMUNITIES NOW, MORE THAN EVER

Communities are, and should be, diverse – and there's a great need for them now. Drinkwater explains: 'Now we see broader challenges in how fragmented and furious the world can be: there's a stronger need than ever to find and contribute to our own communities, online and offline, to remember we're stronger together.'

Communities are powerful, and tapping into them can make a huge difference to your idea and the support you receive as you grow. In the early stages, you might be working with a community of people who share the problem you're solving – they could meet online in a Facebook or WhatsApp group you coordinate, or be reached in an email list. Go where your users are and use existing platforms to communicate with them.

For anyone building a community, Drinkwater advises that: 'the most important thing to remember is that you don't own that group. That's why it's important to start with listening. Recognise and celebrate difference, and work to co-create shared values and boundaries.'

MEASURING LOVE WITH PIRATE METRICS

In the classic illustrated children's book, nutbrown hares compete to *Guess How Much I Love You*.[84] Measuring how much people love your product doesn't involve hopping high or going to the moon and back, but measuring engagement.

Building a passionate audience isn't all touchy-feely woolliness, but a matter of metrics, and there are lots of ways to measure love. Pirate Metrics offers a simple structure for measuring each stage of the growth cycle.[85] Its acronym AARRR (say it in your best pirate accent) prompts you to find a metric to measure engagement as you grow. It stands for:

- **Acquisition**. This initial step is when a visitor first arrives on your doorstep, real or virtual. They might land on your website or drop by your stall or shop. You measure their engagement through time spent on webpages or browsing your products. You can monitor the reverse too: how quickly they leave, so-called abandon, or 'bounce', rates.

- **Activation**. Someone tries your product or service. You've converted them from a browser to someone acting, such as by signing up to your newsletter, joining a waitlist, taking a free trial, tasting food, trying on clothes or using your product.

- **Retention**. Once they have tried it, they come back again, and again. You can measure repeat visits and what people do when they return. Figure out what people are actually doing and how they are interacting.

- **Referral**. This is where growth really kicks in, when users recommend your product or service to other people – for example, by sharing it on social networks or giving out a coupon or discount code. When referral works, you can go viral (and achieve growth like Howard Kingston at the top of the chapter). Monitor when new referral customers are first acquired and activated.

- **Revenue**. Finally, the exciting one! Track how many people pay, how much they pay, whether they make repeat payments such as multiple buys or subscriptions, or whether they buy additional features or products – upsells. Once you get revenue, you can monitor your customer acquisition costs and lifetime value, which will show whether you've got a sustainable business model.

Let's see this in action.

HOW A SCHOOLBOY MASTERED GROWTH WITH DATA

George Burgess was studying for his A levels when he launched his first revision app. It was the first term of the new school year, and, as November hit, he dropped it in the App Store and sat back to watch download figures.

'That was where I made my first big error,' Burgess says. 'I hadn't done any marketing or PR. I just stuck it up there and hoped that other kids would find it. I was getting tens of downloads a day.'

While Burgess was, he says, a student first and an entrepreneur second, he still expected more of a response. But getting a few downloads was enough to challenge him to do more and figure out how to expand his reach.

He asked himself: what is the secret to app success? That question prompted a series of experiments that drove his acquisition and growth channels and led to his app being used by one in three students in the UK studying for their GCSE exams.

BEWARE VANITY METRICS

'I initially went after PR opportunities,' he says. 'I was really hustling back then. I was calling every journalist I could find in local press and national press and anyone who might take an interest.'

Burgess was PR gold – a teenager launching a business in an emerging tech startup field, while still at school (and making PR calls on breaks between lessons and even in the classroom). The press loved him, and he got lots of coverage, which was all very exciting.

But, he explains: 'Press, it turns out, doesn't really drive app downloads. In fact, it hardly moved the needle at all, because the people those publications were reaching were not kids that would be downloading the product. That was learning in itself.'

PR can be the ultimate vanity metric if you're not careful; it becomes coverage for the sake of headlines, rather than to acquire users. Burgess learnt that to reach your audience you need to go where they are.

Getting people to use your product is hard, and you must try a whole bunch of approaches – testing and measuring, abandoning the approaches that fail, and doubling down on those that work. Burgess describes this approach as organic, and admits to not knowing what he was doing when he started, but he persisted and tried different routes to market until one paid off: partnerships.

It was a discussion with his geography teacher that gave him the idea. His teacher Mr Williams was helping him write content for the app, when he suggested talking to publishers who already had content. Like a good school kid set a piece of homework by a favourite teacher, Burgess was on it.

'I started calling and emailing different publishing firms. The largest educational publisher in the world is Pearson. I literally emailed info@pearson and said, "I'm building revision apps. I've had a minor amount of success. I'd love to talk to you about this." Somehow that email found itself in front of the director of BBC Active, which is the joint venture between Pearson and BBC Worldwide who published the BBC Bitesize revision guides.'

Burgess was invited to a meeting at their offices on the Strand in London; he pitched a partnership, and soon lawyers were checking the legality of getting a teenager to sign a contract. Just after his eighteenth birthday, the deal was done, and he had a route to growth. But it was no overnight success; it took years of working with publishers and building apps for them to really understand the market and how it works.

After three years, Burgess pivoted the business away from partnerships back to building his own app again – Gojimo was finally born. He raised £750,000 in investment and planned a huge launch, only to realise – for a second time – that PR coverage in the wrong places does not drive downloads!

'The key to the success,' Burgess says, 'is building a quality product, then figuring out the marketing and growth angle.'

This is where product/market fit matters. You must have the right product for the right market to get growth. Burgess was now 21, at the helm of an investment-backed company, but he was still learning. While Gojimo was getting hundreds of downloads, Burgess admits: 'We very quickly learnt that we hadn't got the product right. We realised the users just weren't engaged enough. They weren't sticking around.'

It took Burgess and his team another year to crack the problem of engaging users and getting them to stick around. They did it with data.

DOUBLE DOWN ON DATA

Pirate Metrics comprises five stages of measuring growth. While Burgess knew he still had to master the first two steps – acquisition and activation – the real challenge was retention – getting users to use and keep using Gojimo. It doesn't matter how many people download your app if all they do is abandon it; it's nothing but a leaky bucket, and any money or effort you put behind acquisition is lost. Download metrics are another vanity metric if no one is using your product.

Burgess stopped focussing on download stats and instead got better at understanding what customers were doing with Gojimo. 'We had very specific data points for watching,' he says. 'Only when we were happy with them did we really start to spend money and pay attention to marketing. Like any other digital marketing, it was all in trial and error, testing different channels, looking at what the conversion rates were, looking at how much it was costing us.'

By looking at the data and monitoring specific metrics, the team at Gojimo had evidence of what was working as they iterated the product and tested the marketing. It may have taken a year, but when they figured it out, the results were amazing. It all came down to understanding who they were building the app for, and then really getting to know that group's pain points.

That's what Burgess did. 'Every sixteen year old does their GCSEs in May in the UK. We were leveraging this pain point.' They used Facebook ads to reach the students, offering Gojimo as a free tool. He says:

'It was a no-brainer. It's like: "Here's something free to use on that mobile phone you're already using for four hours a day that will help you pass those painful exams that are coming up in three weeks' time." The click-through rate was massive, particularly when we were doing it the month before their exam. The cost for acquisition was extraordinarily low because the ads we were putting up were relevant to nine out of ten of the kids who were seeing them.'

Gojimo was tapping into a problem that students faced, and offered a solution that worked. It had product/market fit and smashed all the markers of a viral hit: Gojimo was trending on Twitter, it was a top keyword search term, and it broke into the top ten on the App Store. Students and teachers loved it.

FEEL THE LOVE

As well as hitting big milestones, Burgess remembers the emails from students saying: 'I've learnt more from this app than from my teacher all year,' 'I got my A because of this app,' or 'I passed my GCSE because of Gojimo.'

That kind of feedback has a big impact: it makes you realise you are doing something that helps people and motivates you to do more.

'Making a difference in people's lives,' Burgess says, 'as corny as that sounds, to have an app that at least one in three kids are using and they rate on average four and a half stars and they send you emails and tweets just to say how useful it's been, that's what made me fall in love with the education sector. I went into EdTech by mistake. I ended up loving it.'

The key to successful measurement is to find one metric at each stage and treat it like a brainstorm: notice different behaviours, and monitor them in ways that are as measurable and tangible as possible. Change the metrics you're looking at if the first ones aren't giving you any useful information. Remember – it's all about experimenting.

Try it now. Think about how people come to you and how they interact once they've arrived. Work through each stage of the Pirate Metrics to come up with a few different ways you could measure that engagement and figure out what data you can gather.

A MOUNTAIN TO SCALE?

When you read stories like that of Howard Kingston, who grew *I Am Playr* from zero users to 20 million in eighteen months, it feels like you're not just contemplating a mountain to climb, but a sheer cliff face to scale. Which, after all, is what hockey stick growth most closely resembles.

Don't feel daunted. You can do this.

Having a happy hustle is all about taking small steps so you can move quickly and adjust what you do without wasting time, effort and money that you don't have. It's about feeling good about the progress you are making and learning from when it goes wrong. Acknowledge any feelings of self-doubt and counter them with action. Learn, try different things, keep motivated.

Small steps can lead to significant growth, which is the experience Kingston had:

> 'We were testing loads, constantly putting in new things and changing things. One of the things might've been updating the website, or putting in different buttons in the app. So many things that I don't remember! We had a backlog, and we were rolling out new things. And then we brought in the share with five friends; that was just something that worked really, really well.'

Kingston learnt that no one knows exactly what will cause an idea to go viral and scale. He explains: 'I think the biggest lesson, actually, is you have to expect that most stuff won't work. You need to go into it expecting most of the ideas will fail.'

Rather than get disheartened, we too can follow his advice to keep trying out new things, tweaking what's there and all the time measuring the results. For *I Am Playr*, this had a huge impact on user growth, but it also had a profound impact on Kingston himself.

'I grew up on a farm in Ireland – *so* not California,' Kingston says. I'd started businesses before, but they were quite local. I'd never been close to making something go global before, and that experience has fundamentally shifted my mind in terms of what's possible; if you broaden your focus beyond a local concern, you can grow by 80,000 customers a day – for free.'

Your personal experience is the starting point for building a community and growing an audience. Take your family memories, or your childhood or school experiences, and use them, however small or local they might feel. Keep focussed on what people like and love now, and build your community from there. Take one step at a time to climb the mountain.

CHAPTER SUMMARY

- **In short**: Work with a small community to reach product/market fit for your idea.

- **Start now**: Find two or three 'passionate enthusiasts' to form the basis of your community.

- **Go expert**: Apply Pirate Metrics – from acquisition through to retention.

- **Be happy**: Align ambition for your idea with your audience by determining how big is big enough.

- **Next step**: You're ready to accelerate your hustle.

CHAPTER TWELVE

Hustle

When I grow up I would like to be a nurse. I would like the nurse's uniform. Nurses help people if they are sick. I would like to save up my money for a big shiny car.

When my sister-in-law Jane Haslett-Evans was five years old and was asked what she wanted to be when she grew up, she had laser focus on her future self.

Not only did she get a gold star for sharing her dream, she grew up to fulfil this ambition and now works as a clinical research nurse at Christie Hospital, an international leader in cancer research and development. She had a dream, she worked towards her goal throughout school, college and many years of training, and made it happen. (Although she's still waiting for the big shiny car.)

Haslett-Evans has a 'calling' – work that is rewarding in its own right and contributes to something more significant than her own needs.[86] Amy Wrzesniewski, associate professor of organizational behaviour at Yale University's School of Management, found that people divide into one of three distinct attitudes towards their work:[87]

- **Job**. The reward is purely financial. A job might pay the bills, but you're living for the weekend, your hobbies and side projects.

- **Career**. There's deeper personal investment, but your focus is on putting in long hours to achieve more money, promotions and higher social standing.

- **Calling**. Work is inseparable from life; it's intrinsically rewarding in its own right, not just as a means to an end. You contribute to a higher value or something bigger than yourself.

It's a useful framework as you figure out how your idea fits into your life, whether you want a fun side project over the summer months, a classic side hustle that makes a bit of extra cash, or the opportunity to build a multimillion-dollar business that will help a billion people. Each path requires different actions: the first needs some spare time for a few days or weeks, the last involves a global problem that requires venture capital money to solve.

What do you want to be when you grow up? What do you want your idea to be when it grows up?

SIDE HUSTLE OR STARTUP?

Having a calling like Haslett-Evans brings great fulfilment and has the side benefit of leading to better health – quite a bonus when working in healthcare. Wrzesniewski and her fellow researchers found that what contributes most to life satisfaction is not which category of work people fall into, but how they see their own work. In short, your personal values matter more to your happiness than external signifiers, such as income or occupational prestige. Figuring out what you want will lead to better outcomes and, dare I say it, happiness.

Hands up – I had no idea what I wanted to be when I grew up. Even at my fully grownup current age, I still don't know exactly. My approach is to figure it out by trying different things and seeing what works and what I enjoy. Don't worry if you're not sure whether you're starting a side hustle or a startup; the next chapter will help.

Your idea is starting to take off. You've built, tested and grown an audience. Now, you need to keep it going. It's time to hustle. Find out how to:

- Balance your time at work with a side hustle.

- Bootstrap your business full-time.

- Use an accelerator to boost your startup.

- Get investment from angels and VCs.

ALL ABOUT THE HUSTLE

You're no stranger to hustling. Back in Chapter 8 you persuaded people to part with their pennies to validate your idea.

Let's take a step back and see what it means to have a side hustle. Over to master of the side hustle, Chris Guillebeau, who is evangelical about the benefits.[88] He's right, there's so much to gain from balancing a side project alongside your job: it gives you a foundation for experimentation while reducing the risk of going all-in on an untested business venture; you get an additional source of income, which reduces your dependency on a single employer; you learn new skills and get a creative outlet; and it's fun. He says:

> 'Starting a side hustle is like "playing entrepreneurially" without making a huge commitment. The stakes are low and the potential is high.'[89]

A side hustle was my route into entrepreneurship. I did my initial research and validation while working full-time, then moved to a part-time job so I could spend more time making my idea happen. It's how many people start out.

Anne-Marie Imafidon, creator of Stemettes, was told by an advisor not to leave her job until you 'literally can't do both anymore.' She clung to this advice for two years. Imafidon says: 'As much as Stemettes might be cool, and as much as we have so much fun in the office, I shouldn't move across until I literally don't have enough hours in the day to breathe – only then consider going full-time.'

When I asked her if that was the right decision, she said that a small part of her wishes she'd done it sooner! When you see what she's achieved with Stemettes, it's amazing she had any time for her day job: she got funding, launched and ran multiple events and a mentoring scheme, advised the government, and met the queen and the prime minister before setting out her stall as a full-time startup founder. Now she's CEO and 'Head Stemette'; she has a team to help her achieve her mission, with an app, a documentary and a TV series in the pipeline.

While Imafidon ultimately left her day job, others decide to stick with it and start up a business on the side.

YOU CAN DO BOTH

'I think it's important for people to realise,' says Gunita Bhasin, 'you can do this alongside your full-time job.'

Bhasin is a startup founder with a job. She's proof that you can do both. Bhasin was working a demanding job in banking when she had an idea. She played around with early versions, teaching herself the skills she needed to bring her idea to life.

'As soon as I realised this is something I want to develop,' says Bhasin, 'I first taught myself how to code. Then I did this part-time course in product management, once a week in the evening. I'd work on it evenings, weekends – I would say, ten hours a week.'

Motivated by passion for her idea, Bhasin learnt how to manage a side hustle alongside a full-time job. She researched, created and tested Showcased, an app that allows people to launch their own side hustles, by connecting them to resources related to their passions. The mobile app helps people take their passions to the next level. She explains:

> 'First, you select your passions that you want to work on. You decide when you will collaborate

with other people on these passions. Then you start to showcase your passions. The idea of showcasing is really to create social proof. When you showcase something, you inherently start to position yourself as somebody who's good at a specific field. For example, you can showcase your startup on the app and people might reach out to you to find out more about what you offer.'

In the same way her idea champions collaboration, Bhasin admits she could not have done it alone. She found two co-founders to get her idea to launch. Together they share a passion. Bhasin says: 'What we tried to build is something that empowers people to take that first step and work with other people on making their passion happen. That's exactly what we did, as well, in terms of launching this and getting it off the ground.'

She uses her free time to work on the startup. 'We have our signature Sunday night calls every week with the founding team,' Bhasin says, 'to discuss how development was progressing and what each of us had worked on that week.'

TRADE-OFFS

Working full-time while being a startup founder is not an easy feat.

It definitely has its disadvantages. For one, it takes longer to build something, and then there's the fact that you can't access support through many startup accelerators because you've got a full-time job. It takes tenacity and persistence. You also need a supportive employer, as Bhasin explains:

'My team at work realised that working on this startup helped me contribute better as an employee, because I had a better understanding of some of the things the firm is going through. Working on the startup helps me keep more satisfied. On days when things aren't going well, I'm doing all these other things that I'm passionate about, so that I have this personal satisfaction and fulfilment. I feel as though the startup makes my life a lot more meaningful.'

Bhasin was lucky to have a supportive employer. If you're going to fit your hustle around the day job, there's one golden rule: don't take the micky.

According to *Inc.* magazine, 71 per cent of founders said the idea for their company was based on a problem they faced in a previous job. Workplaces are a breeding ground for ideas, but beware! If you're hustling during work hours, it could be owned by your employer. Check your contract for clauses on intellectual property before you use your work computer to knock up a business plan.

Keep your side projects away from your desk and in your own time – lunchtime and breaks should be fine. And remember, multitasking leads to poorer outcomes, so don't let both your job and side hustle suffer as you flit between the two.

It's not easy having a side hustle, but Bhasin made smart choices about her job which gave her the space to make her idea happen, and now she's sharing her passion to get other people's projects started.

Bhasin mentions one final benefit to working while hustling: she could keep control of her idea by funding it herself. She says: 'Having job security makes it possible for me to invest my own money in the startup, which is really good.'

That's what we'll come to next: the necessary business of funding your idea and the options available to make it happen.

BOOTSTRAPPING

I was working full-time when I kicked off my side project, fitting it in on evenings, weekends and days off. I then decided to go part-time, working three and a half days for a publisher and three and a half days to get Prolifiko off the ground.

I didn't have the balance right – working seven days a week is not sustainable. I had enough proof that it was working, and I was desperate to spend more time on it. So, I resigned.

I negotiated a six-month notice period, and over that time I squirrelled away every penny I earned after the bills were paid. That gave me enough savings to live for six months once I was out of employment. I lived very frugally.

Over the years, I have bootstrapped in every way possible – from selling my stuff on eBay, to taking consultancy work, to accepting the odd tenner from my Dad for treats (and once a more substantial wodge when cashflow was non-existent and he subbed my rent – thanks, Dad, I owe you big time). There have been loans, grants and investment from the startup accelerator Ignite. Keeping going is tough, as we're about to hear.

This is not advice, Dr Mohammad Al-Ubaydli tells me straight and clear. 'Do not,' he says, 'do this at home.' The founder of Patients Know Best, the patient-controlled online medical records company, Dr Al-Ubaydli explains the cost of getting his idea up and running:

'In the first five years, we never had more than two months working runway. I don't mean it as a point of pride or romance. I mean, you really shouldn't do this unless you cannot think of anything else you want to do. You have to feel compelled to do it. By far the most likely outcome is you'll go bankrupt while the market is learning about you or about why it needs this. The tactic is to stay alive for as long as possible. Keep overheads as low as possible. Be as efficient as possible. Extend your runway any way that you can.'

YOU NEED RUNWAY TO LAUNCH

'Runway' is my favourite startup slang because it's such a perfect metaphor. If you're a pilot, and your runway is too short, your plane will fail to take off, and will crash. The same is true when you're getting an idea off the ground. The reason most startups fail is because their runway disappears before they've had time to launch their product.

Jon Bradford is the 'Godfather of European accelerators': he has created the support, structure, advice and funding for thousands of startups. He's got the perfect vantage point to tell us what to do now.

'While it might be a cliché, it is very true – if you are not embarrassed by your first product, you have built too much.'

Bradford has seen startups launch into the stratosphere and watched as others crashed and burned. He says it all comes down to runway: 'Many entrepreneurs spend 80 per cent of their time building a product before engaging with potential customers, leaving only 20 per cent of their runway to respond and react to feedback.'

You know the importance of making something people want, engaging with potential customers as you develop, test and build your idea. You've got this far, but you still have further to go before you launch. For your concept to take off, you need to fill your tank.

Dr Al-Ubaydli kept his runway just long enough to launch and grow a global company. There were countless sleepless nights as he worried about more than just the financial costs of keeping going.

'One of the things that worried me,' says Dr Al-Ubaydli, 'is I've seen friends in the process of starting a company divorce their partners because they spent too much time in the company and not with their family. If you lose the company that's bad. If you lose the family that's terrible.' He was determined that family came first, which was put to the test early on when his wife, the breadwinner in the family, became pregnant with twins.

Dr Al-Ubaydli refers to his wife Laura as his 'first investor': she kept the family going financially for three years while he got Patients Know Best up and running. He might have been a solo founder, but they were a partnership and she was the only one with a salary. They agreed red lines together – for example, not taking on any debt – and sat down each month to review how it was going. At their monthly meeting, they looked at what money they had coming in, they planned childcare, and they looked at sales and customer feedback to see if the company was going in the right direction – whether it would become sustainable.

Having a family to look after made Dr Al-Ubaydli prioritise his time. He explains: 'I tried to get rid of anything that would take time away from the family. In the beginning that was commuting. From day one I worked from home.' That decision ended up being a good recruitment move: he could attract staff who wanted flexible or home working. The company is still a virtual team, now with 55 employees from twelve different countries. Making decisions aligned with his personal values, and focussing on his vision and customer needs, he survived and built a sustainable business that attracted investment.

It's time to talk investment. What follows is pretty focussed on traditional startups, but you'll find relevant advice here, whatever your hustle. We'll untangle the mysterious world of angel investment and venture capital, but first, let's look at accelerators.

THE STARTUP ACCELERATOR

'A good accelerator can have a profound impact upon a startup at its earliest stage,' says Jon Bradford.

Accelerators typically back early-stage founders who have validated their idea and have some proof of success, such as a minimal viable product, some users or some revenue. This is exactly where you're at.

Bradford earned his 'Godfather' nickname after launching the first accelerator boot camp outside of the US. He stimulated a vibrant ecosystem across Europe that supports early-stage businesses and the communities they're based in. He takes a 'give first' philosophy to encourage and support others who have similar aspirations to launch accelerators. Let's look at what this involves.

A startup accelerator is defined as 'a fixed-term, cohort-based programme, including mentorship and educational components, that culminates in a public pitch event or demo-day.'[90] The original model came from Silicon Valley where private investment funds take *equity* (a share of your company's future value) in exchange for seed investment (initial funding). Since the early days, programmes have proliferated, with thousands of companies and public bodies setting up accelerators globally.

By giving you both money and expert advice, startup accelerators can advance your idea in leaps and bounds. However, it can be tricky to figure out which one will help your idea and which will distract you, slow down your progress and destroy your idea. Let's ask Bradford for his advice in navigating this ecosystem.

From the moment your idea hits the world, the clock starts ticking. 'The limiting factor,' says Bradford, 'is time and money. If a startup fails to make sufficient progress within this constraint, it will neither attract investment nor customers, ultimately leading to its failure.'

This is where accelerators can help. He explains: 'Accelerators leverage resources, networks and experienced mentors to "do more, faster", which a startup would not be able to achieve on their own.'

A good accelerator will help you to, well, accelerate your idea. The data backs this up – the top programmes help startups reach key milestones such as growth, investment and exit much faster. They are also more likely to cause your startup to fail faster – tough, but essential if you're planning a business.

Bradford advises: 'It is important for a startup to do its research before joining an accelerator: speaking to alumni of the programme that might have been successful or otherwise.'

He's right, the proliferation of accelerators has resulted in very few having any positive impact, with many actually slowing down a startup's progress.[91] If you've got an accelerator in your sights, take time to hit the internet and contact companies who've been through that process.

HOW TO GET A PLACE WITH A TOP ACCELERATOR

If you've decided accelerators are right for you, then how do you go about getting a place on a good one?

The first accelerator was started in 2005 in Cambridge, Massachusetts. Called Y Combinator, it was founded by Paul Graham, Jessica Livingston, Trevor Blackwell and Robert Tappan Morris. It subsequently moved to Silicon Valley. Y Combinator has funded 1,900 startups, which now have a combined valuation of over $100 billion.[92] Their community of over 4,000 founders includes startup super-companies such as Airbnb, Dropbox, Reddit, Stripe, Twitch and Weebly. It is far and away the most successful accelerator ever, followed by Techstars. Between them, they accept between 1–3 per cent of applicants in a highly competitive field.

While Paul Graham is the public face of Y Combinator, he credits Jessica Livingston with the skills to spot top talent, calling her the 'social radar' because of her ability to judge people. When the founding team interviewed startups for the programme, the three men often focussed on the technical idea, while Livingston observed people. She looked for 'earnest people' to fund, and once said: 'I always tried to create an asshole-free culture. If I could tell someone was a conceited asshole, we didn't fund them.'[93] She was the gatekeeper for who made it into Y Combinator.

The personal qualities of founders are often the best predictor of how a startup will do; so I asked Livingston what she looks for in someone who has an idea, and what skills and attitudes she suggests early-stage entrepreneurs should cultivate.

'The things I look for are determination, focus, empathy for users, flexible-mindedness, a deep relationship with co-founders ... to name a few. But of course, none of these always works out perfectly!'

If you've read this far, you'll be familiar with many of those qualities.

INVESTMENT OPTIONS FROM SEED TO EXIT

Accelerators are known as 'pre-seed funding' – the very first stage of investment in a startup that often hasn't started pulling in revenue yet. A good programme will teach you how to structure your idea as a business and how to raise further investment to help it grow – think of it like school with funding.

As a startup business grows and makes revenue, one option is to take seed funding from an investor. An investor will exchange capital for an equity stake (i.e. shares) in the company. Investment is often given in 'rounds', as follows.

- **Seed funding** is the earliest round and provides money to help a founder prove their idea. Options at this stage include angel investors and crowdfunding.

- **Startup investment** often covers the costs associated with product development and early marketing.

- **Growth funding**, often called a 'Series A' round, is where venture capital firms get involved. This is the stage where sales and user growth really takes off.

- **Subsequent investment** rounds are called Series B, C, D and onwards. The founders' share will get significantly diluted, and more control is handed to the investors. By this stage, the startup will have significant growth, global coverage, and many employees and overheads.

- **Exit** is where the real money is made. The startup will be acquired, or have an initial public offering known as an 'IPO' – this is when the startup goes public and offers shares to other investors.

Like all investment, the funding is a bet on future performance. If the startup goes bust, the investors lose their money. But if the startup gets acquired or goes public, they'll make a lot of money. In some cases, eye-watering amounts of money. The biggest gamblers at the table are venture capitalists (VCs) and playing with these types is a high-risk, high-gain strategy. Before we get to VCs let's consider angels.

ANGEL INVESTMENT

There were very few options available to Alex Depledge when she was looking for investment to grow her vision for Hassle.com, the website to book home cleaners. The startup support ecosystem was limited, as she explains: 'When we started, it felt like there was only VC and that you had to go that way. There are more options for financing around now.'

Other types of funding range from the three 'f's (friends, family and fools), crowdfunding through platforms like Kickstarter or Seedrs, traditional forms of debt available through banks and other loan providers such as Startup Loans, through to angel investment. Angel investment has been particularly helpful to Depledge.

'We have been lucky to have met some amazing angels who have become friends and mentors,' says Depledge. 'Angels tend to be more pragmatic – harder to get on board but easier to manage once you do. They add value and especially contacts. They are also good as a sounding board.'

An angel investor is usually an entrepreneur who invests their own money in startups. Their interest is about more than financial return: offering advice and mentorship on a part-time basis. Depledge admits not all angels are perfect. 'While you do get problematic angels,' she says, 'they tend to be less jumpy and more understanding as former entrepreneurs.'

Because angels have experience of the ups and downs of entrepreneurship, they have empathy for founders and understand the pressure. Plus, as they are investing their own money, they have an interest in how it is spent and will offer advice and a friendly ear.

Since her exit from Hassle.com, Depledge has started a new startup with her previous co-founder

Jules Coleman. Together they created Resi, a platform that uses technology to provide affordable design for people who want to develop, extend or refurbish their house.

They came up with the idea when their own building projects hit the buffers, and realised there had to be a better way. They had a hunch that technology could disrupt the architectural industry to provide people with a faster, cheaper product, which still had the quality of a bespoke design.

Depledge and Coleman both invested their own money in Resi, but to really make it work, they needed additional funds. They had learnt from their first investment experience and were selective in who they took money from. Depledge says her new investors: 'had to have a big cheque book, write the money off on investment, and a have a big rolodex. Most importantly they couldn't display any dickish tendencies.'

VENTURE CAPITAL

VCs provide financing to early-stage startups who are considered to have high-growth potential. Like angels, VC firms get equity in exchange for their investment and give expert advice on how to grow and manage the business.

'VCs claim to add value,' Depledge says, 'but I have met very few who actually do. You end up managing the business for them instead of for yourself or your customers. Most second timers I have come across are largely in the mindset of retain control and aim for profits.'

Founding a startup is a learning experience, and serial entrepreneurs get the opportunity to put into practice the stuff they have learnt the hard way. Not accepting investment, she says, is not less ambitious, it just makes sense for many people.

However, if you want to attract VC investment, your idea needs to be innovative, disruptive and have a potentially large market – ideally worth many billions. That's right – your idea needs to be absolutely massive. VCs will then take on the risk of financing in the hope that some of the startups they support will become successful and give them a high rate of return. Be warned, VC investments have high rates of failure, which is why they have a reputation for toughness, and finding the right VC takes a lot of time and effort.

Dr Mohammad Al-Ubaydli told us that for the first five years of his patient-controlled medical records company, Patients Know Best, he never had more than two months working runway. He didn't choose that route; he desperately wanted investment, but it had to be from the right sort of investor.

When he goes to London now, he says: 'At every tube station I get off, I get a flashback from a meeting where someone's turned us down for money. If you can't cope with being rejected, do not go into startups.' When I asked how many investors turned him down, he replies over a hundred. That's a lot of rejection. But it was for all the right reasons, as he and the investors wouldn't have been able to work with one another.

He explains what happened when he pitched these big investment funds:

> 'They would basically say, "It's a great idea, Mohammad. Think how much money you can make selling the patients' data." We would say, "No, it's not our data, it's the patients' data." And they'd look at us like we had no idea what

we were doing. Those weren't going to be the right investors. They weren't going to be aligned with our mission. It was really hard to see them lose interest after this because we had no money.'

Imagine that you've living month to month, with little or no runway: the pressure to take investment must be huge. But you cannot compromise the principles behind what you are trying to do. The whole purpose of Patients Know Best is that it is patient-controlled – the data is the patients' and theirs alone. Dr Al-Ubaydli kept going, and eventually he got funded when Balderton Capital, one of Europe's top three VCs, invested £3.5 million.

'The flip side,' he says, 'is when we did find the right investors, you could tell instantly this was the right time. It was so worth the wait.'

When you talk to founders who seek investment, they say you must 'kiss a lot of frogs'. For Dr Al-Ubaydli it was 100. George Burgess, founder of student revision app Gojimo, tallied up 300. Both found their suitors eventually.

No one can tell you whether you need to take investment, or when you should take it, but whatever route you take, you need runway to keep going. Calculate if you can survive long enough to grow, get your head around basic financial planning like a cash flow forecast, and consider all the options from side hustling, to bootstrapping, joining an accelerator, or taking investment from angels and VCs.

Runway is about more than money; you need support to keep you going.

Next we'll cover building a support system and a network that avoids the 'dickish' people Depledge warned about. Read on to find your people and the possibility of happiness.

CHAPTER SUMMARY

- **In short**: You need runway to launch your idea.

- **Start now**: Think about what sort of an idea you want to build and consider the financing options.

- **Go expert**: Check out accelerators and other forms of seed financing.

- **Be happy**: Keep aligned with your values and whether you have a calling or hobby.

- **Next step**: Build your happy-making support network.

Conclusion: Happy

George Bettany was feeling jealous. His first company had folded, and he was back to a regular job. While the perks of a stable wage were great, he was envious of other startups – not the success that other founders were having, but their relationships. Bettany missed working with James Routledge, his best friend and co-founder of his first company.

It's no wonder he was feeling out of sorts. Relationships are the significant contributing factor to our overall happiness, as psychologists Carolyn Murray and Jean Peacock observe:

> 'Contrary to the belief that happiness is hard to explain, or that it depends on having great wealth, researchers have identified the core factors in a happy life. The primary components are number of friends, closeness of friends, closeness of family and relationships with co-workers and neighbors. Together these features explain about 70 per cent of personal happiness.'[94]

It was truth time – Bettany had to tell Routledge. He explains: 'I remember going to dinner with him and talking through, "What do you want in your life? What do you want the business to be? Where are you at with girlfriends and relationships?" We talked about everything and, luckily, he had the same vision as well.'

They went on to co-found Sanctus, the startup whose vision is to put a mental health gym on every high street. Bettany describes working together again as easy – they just slotted back together. The second time around was better because they had learnt from their first startup and were older, wiser and more balanced.

'The last company,' says Bettany, 'we didn't really think about the mission we were on, the vision that we had. And that caught up with us. When you lay those foundations and you're really clear up front, it just sets it up from day one.'

For some friends, the longer they work together the stronger the relationships. Take Jules Coleman and Alex Depledge who met at work, went on to co-found Hassle.com with a third friend, and then set up Resi together after they had sold Hassle.com. Coleman says: 'There's nothing like running a business together to become best friends. It would feel very weird to start something without Alex.'[95]

Others co-found with partners. In the last chapter, we met Jessica Livingston who co-founded Y Combinator with her husband Paul Graham and two friends. We also heard how Dr Mohammad Al-Ubaydli called his wife his first investor. Likewise, my first investor was my husband – to begin with that meant money and support, but soon he was doing more of the work, and we became co-founders. Now you can't tell where the ideas originate. Together our business is stronger.

While relationships are important to our overall happiness, they also contribute to the success of your hustle. Working with someone you know can be a big bonus if you take time to be honest and build the business with shared values. Don't worry if you don't have friends and family in the front line – there are other ways to build a support network. Having peers and mentors around you to ask for advice and support can supercharge your idea.

This concluding chapter is all about finding the happy in your hustle and starts with looking at people who can help you make your idea happen, including:

- Finding a mentor to advise you.

- Building a support network of peers.

- Developing the grit needed to keep going.

- How to find your personal happy hustle.

THE SUM OF THE PEOPLE YOU SPEND TIME WITH

A few years ago, researchers found that obesity is contagious among friends. The study looked at a large social network of 12,067 people, who they followed for 32 years; it found that, within mutual friendships, if your friend becomes obese, your chance of becoming obese increases by 171 per cent.[96] It also found an increased risk up to three degrees of separation – your friends' friends of friends. This is down to something called the network phenomena, where traits spread through social ties.

You can use this effect to help you. There's a saying that 'you are the sum of the five people you spend the most time with.' When I managed the writers' retreat centre, I would see the positive effect that being surrounded by writers for a week had on people. No one was interested in what people did for a living, where they lived, what they earned – instead they asked what they were writing, about the details of plot or character. It was, for many people, the first time they identified themselves as writers. It gave them permission *to be* a writer.

You have permission to be what you want to be; so find the people who can help you. If your family and friends aren't able to offer you support, or don't help you to see yourself in this new role, then reach out to others on a similar journey, join a network or group. You could even create your own community.

Building a support network early on can make all the difference to your success and happiness. Like IDEO design director Jenn Maer said: 'It's hard to be the only panda in the zoo. You need your people.' She was talking about the power of collaboration for creative thinking, but it applies to all areas of life and work.

While an idea might originate from one person's imagination, it is made stronger by working with other people. As you grow your idea into a concept and business, working with others or drawing on a support network will make both you and your idea stronger. The 'solopreneur' doesn't have to be lonely.

THE MENTOR RELATIONSHIP

When I first had an inkling of an idea for what became Prolifiko, I had no one around me who could provide the right kind of support. So, one of the first things I did was join Ada's List, an online community for women in tech. I could post questions in a safe place and get advice from people who had been through it before. It gave me the confidence to get into tech, a field that had felt completely beyond my skill set and comfort zone. It was also where I found my first mentor, Sally Lait.

I posted a brief on Ada's List for a technology review, and Lait, who runs digital consultancy Records Sound the Same, was one of the consultants who applied. She won the contract, completed the work, and because her insight was so valuable we kept in touch. We checked in each month – I would call on her tech know-how and advice for a whole range of issues, and over time the relationship shifted from consultant/client to mentor/mentee.

Having a mentor made a huge difference, especially in the early days when I was figuring things out. It was important for me to be able ask stupid questions, without being judged, and not feel patronised when things were explained.

In the startup world there's a lot of bravado – everyone is 'crushing it' all the time – but that's bullshit. Accept what you don't know, ask for help, get advice and learn.

Lait is a big fan of the low-key mentoring approach, where she's commissioned not to complete a task on behalf of someone, but to instead coach them to build the skills and knowledge to do it themselves. And the exchange goes both ways, as she says:

> 'While we originally set out down the path of a typical client and project relationship, I was so glad that things shifted over time. I may have mentored Bec through the more technical side of her business' evolution, but through our chats I also learnt a lot about the startup world, and gained someone who I was also able to speak openly to about my own situation and received a lot of support. I'm so pleased that I was able to help Bec build up her skills and knowledge, but I definitely benefited a huge amount from our conversations myself!'[97]

The best mentors take an attitude of life-long learning, always reaching out to learn from their networks. Take Sarah Drinkwater, a world-class expert on community building; she's an advocate of mentoring, both as a mentee and as a mentor.

'Nothing makes me happier than opening doors,' Drinkwater says. 'Mentoring, like coaching, often involves asking the right questions to help unlock what the founder or individual wants and knows: while a mentor can make suggestions, they never know best. It's incredibly fulfilling to help someone figure out how to unbury what they wanted all along.'

Mentoring is one of the most powerful ways you can supercharge your skills. As Jon Bradford says, the mentoring available through a good accelerator helps early-stage startups to 'do more, faster'. And it's more than just a quick fuel-injection – the benefit will keep you flying in the long term by creating a network of wise and supportive people who will always be there for you.

MAKING THE MOST OF A MENTORING RELATIONSHIP

There's no one-size-fits-all approach to building a great mentoring relationship, but there are approaches that work. Finding the right person is often the hardest part – you know you need support but don't know how or where to find a mentor. It will take time, so be patient, do your research, and reach out to people for advice and recommendations. Use an experimental approach similar to working on an idea: sound out various people for advice and choose the best fit based on your needs and wants.

Meet them

Because of the nature of the relationship, you should meet face to face or have a video call first. Ask for a specific piece of advice – don't just say 'let's meet for a coffee' – you need to have something to talk about. Follow up! Build the relationship so you can see if it might work for more formal mentoring.

Agree details

When you've brokered the subject of entering a mentoring arrangement, talk about what's involved – time, frequency, follow-up.

Set goals

Be clear what you hope to get from each session – be honest about your long-term goals and what you need. Prepare in advance, make it easy for your mentor to give you their best advice, tell them what's on your mind and how they can help.

Feedback

Mentoring is a relationship based on trust, honesty and good communication. It's up to you what advice you follow, but offer feedback to your mentor, especially if something they suggested has made a difference.

Invest

Some mentoring relationships last a lifetime, so take time to find someone who is right for you and invest in making it work. The benefits can be huge.

Don't kick your heels while you wait to find the perfect mentor; keep learning from available resources, read blogs and books, and listen to podcasts. If you're looking for specific skill support, sign up for courses and email lists. Join online forums and go to meetups, talks, events and conferences. Who knows, in the same way that creative ideas can appear when you least expect them, you might stumble across your ideal mentor when you're looking elsewhere.

A PERSONAL BOARD OF DIRECTORS

You can get advice without having a formal mentoring agreement. Talking to experts informally is a great way to learn and get support without committing long-term. That's exactly what Anne-Marie Imafidon does.

'I'm very good with asking people that I know and respect for help,' says Imafidon. When she bumps into someone she knows, she'll pose a question. She gets amazing answers – people love to offer advice. Over time, this has built up such that she has a network of advisors. She explains:

> 'I have a brain trust – it's a bit like a personal board of directors. Different people who I respect, who were a little bit further ahead of where I was but who I could bounce ideas off. Whether it's having them as official mentors or informal mentors, or people that I just ask questions.'

The advisor model is replicated in Stemettes, where they have 'Godmothers' who help the organisation. If you have a question you're puzzling over, or a concern about what's next, then make like Imafidon and reach out to people. Be both brave and vulnerable enough to ask for advice and help.

Go along to meetups or join an existing community. Mastermind groups are peer-to-peer mentoring where members help each other with advice to solve problems. A version within the startup community is called 'a good meal with 9others', where local entrepreneurs and startup founders come together over dinner to discuss and solve business challenges they face. It started in London in 2011 and has grown to a network of over 4,000 entrepreneurs in 45 cities around the world.

You are the sum of the people you spend the most time with, so think about who you surround yourself with. Don't drop your current friends and colleagues, but seek new people who are starting out like you or have already made some progress.

- Who can offer support and advice?

- Where can you find an existing community?

- How can you create a new network?

STORIES OF SUCCESS

'From the outside, there's a success story. I'm that guy that set up a business at school when he was fourteen. I'm that guy who grew it into an international company, running it from a mobile phone from his school bag, and then I went on to build a portfolio, a career, and became a philanthropist, and I teach at all these great international universities, and then I got an MBE. It's pretty cool, right? Wrong.'[98]

Vikas Shah lived an enviable life: by the time he was seventeen he had offices in New York, Manchester, London and Sydney. When the dotcom bubble burst, he bounced back and set up a new business, even more profitable than his first. He was a successful and astute businessman who made a lot of money. But he was also a brilliant actor, who hid his anxiety and depression and became a 'hyper-masculine, hyper-alpha caricature of what an entrepreneur should be like.'

He reached a point where he could no longer cope with this duplicity. Suicide felt like his only option. 'This wasn't the first time I thought about doing something like that, but it was the first time I got this close to succeeding. I approached the edge, and I felt this sense of overwhelming loneliness. I didn't want to go in silence. I just wanted to speak to somebody, anybody.'

Runway is about more than money. If you're not functioning, nothing else will. Your mental health is more important than funding rounds. Shah reached the edge before he found that out.

He called a helpline. Reaching out to another person saved his life and put him on the hard path of rebuilding his life. With help, he was able to write a new story of what success looks like. Over many years, he found ways to quieten his anxiety. He tried medication, therapy, CBT, psychoanalysis – even acupuncture and singing bowls.

Shah figured out how he could feel successful both on the outside and on the inside: 'it's about spending time with the people you love, your friends, your hobbies, your cats.' While his solution might be personal to him, research backs up his experience.

HUMAN FLOURISHING

Martin Seligman, professor of psychology at the University of Pennsylvania, and the founder of positive psychology, studies flourishing – namely, what it takes to lead a life of fulfilment, happiness and meaning.

He considers there to be five core elements of psychological well-being, and it's no surprise that relationships are one of the elements.[99] Seligman advises us to build social connections and focus on key relationships in our life. The other four elements are:

- **Engagement** – doing fulfilling work and having interesting hobbies.

- **Accomplishments** – having ambition, setting realistic goals and celebrating achievements.

- **Meaning** – leading a life of purpose; searching for meaning in what we do.

- **Positive emotion** – optimism, having a positive perspective; feeling pleasure and enjoyment.

Flourishing requires us to do difficult things in order to accomplish goals and feel fulfilled, yet it also involves taking time to find pleasure and positive emotion in aspects of our daily lives.

This is the central dilemma of having a happy hustle: fulfilment lies partly in doing hard things, yet if we focus too much on the difficult tasks, we'll burnout.

There's no getting away from it, creating something new takes time – more time than you imagine when you're starting out. While hacking your way to success might make the headlines, there are no shortcuts –

true excellence takes deliberate practice, often called the 10,000-hour rule. That's about ten years of effort, not quite the overnight success story we might hope for.

When you embark on a new project you get a rush of excitement – a buzz that gets you started but soon fades. To keep going you need to develop perseverance, also known as grit. Professor Angela Duckworth, who works with Seligman in the psychology department of the University of Pennsylvania, studies grit. She describes it as the daily discipline of trying to do things better than we did yesterday. She writes:

'Many of us, it seems, quit what we start far too early and far too often. Even more than the effort a gritty person puts in in a single day, what matters is they wake up the next day, and the next, ready to get on that treadmill and keep going.'[100]

HOW TO KEEP GOING

While it might take 10,000 hours to build expertise, that total is made up of choices we make each day as to how we will spend our time. We might have our eyes on the long-term end goal of success, but true happiness comes from enjoying the journey, as Zen philosopher Alan Watts explains:

'We thought of life by analogy with a journey, a pilgrimage, which had a serious purpose at the end. And the thing was to get to that end – success or whatever it is, maybe heaven after you're dead. But we missed the point the whole way along. It was a musical thing, and you were supposed to sing, or to dance, while the music was being played.'[101]

Whatever stage of the ideas journey you're at, you'll find the happy in your hustle.

It all starts with enjoying what you do. If you're going to work at something for many years it helps if you're interested in it.

Many people worry about finding their passion, as if there is only one passion available to them, and their life is a quest to find it. Relax and enjoy the process of seeking. Go out into the world and try different things, experiment, be curious and develop your interests. Something will spark your attention and give you the enthusiasm to get going.

Take small steps. Don't get overwhelmed by considering the whole journey or achieving an end goal; instead make incremental progress.

Find some time, however little, and use it to work on your idea. At the end of a session, plan the next thing you'll do, so you'll know where to pick up next time. If you get stuck, think of the smallest thing you can do – then do it. Use mind mapping and other free association techniques to work through blocks and generate options.

Have an experimental mindset. Test little and often with real users and use their feedback to refine and hone your idea.

Build in time to reflect and learn. When things go wrong, work out how to do it better in the future. Celebrate when things go well. This will give you the perseverance and grit to keep going.

Find people who can help at each stage: ask friends and peers to get involved in brainstorms or build and test prototypes. Working with people in your target market will build communities of people who are really into what you do. One day you'll have customers who love your idea so much they will pay for it or investors who will support you financially.

Have empathy for your users. Thinking of what you're creating for them will bring conviction that what you're doing matters – not just to you but to others. If you're solving a problem for other people, you can connect to their needs and wants to find purpose and meaning in your journey.

Be optimistic. Duckworth found that hope defines what it takes to have grit. She says:

> 'From the very beginning to the very end, it is inestimably important to learn to keep going even when things are difficult, even when we have doubts. At various points, in big ways and small, we get knocked down. If we stay down, grit loses. If we get up, grit prevails.'

LIVE YOUR PERSONAL HAPPY HUSTLE

This book is your companion for the journey.

The end notes are full of notes and indexes to help you research and plan. There are indexes of the illustrations, exercises and expert stories. Dip back in as you hustle to seek practical guidance and inspiration.

While you can use various metrics to determine the success of your idea, whether you have the right solution to a problem, or how well you're growing and reaching the market, the metrics for a happy hustle are personal. Only you can define your success. It all starts by starting.

So, what are you waiting for? It's time to find your happy hustle.

TOOLS AND TOP TIPS INDEX

Chapter 8

Chapter 9

Chapter 10

Illustration Index

Original illustrations in the book by Cara Holland, unless otherwise indicated.

Story Index

Conclusion

Acknowledgements

While writing is a solitary process, making a book is truly collaborative and involves many people and many cycles of iteration. Like many ideas, this book started small, first as a workshop then a series of blogs. The prototype was a nine-page proposal brought to life by Alison Jones's proposal challenge. After she got me off the starting blocks, Alison provided the support, advice and cheerleading to keep me going – I cannot thank her enough.

Once the concept was in the world, it received validation from many people. My agent Michael Alcock encouraged me to pitch the idea to publishers whose professional feedback shaped what the book would become. Michael sold my idea, guided negotiations and shielded me from rejection. He found the perfect publisher in Icon Books, who have supported my approach to innovation and collaboration in the writing process.

The Icon dream team is led by editor Kiera Jamison, an editorial goddess who brings wisdom, wit and insight (and the best side notes). Kiera has levelled up my writing – I could not have done it without her. Thank you to team Icon, especially Andrew Furlow, Lucy Cooper, Lydia Wilson and Victoria Reed for championing the book and supporting experimentation and testing. Thanks to Ruth Killick for her publicity expertise and endless enthusiasm; James Jones whose brilliant cover design nailed the feeling of the book; Cecile Berbesi who created the text design and typeset the book; and Cara Holland who illustrated the book with humour, and was my writing buddy throughout the process, reading early drafts and offering feedback and regular pep talks.

Many people helped with early research – thank you to Alison Coward, Claire Merrick, Gabi Matic, Joe Scarboro, Laura Bennet, Matt Roberts, Matt Trinetti, Nicole

Yershon, Sam Fisher and Tash Willcocks for your advice, introductions and guidance.

I am grateful to all my interviewees for taking the time to share their wisdom and stories of success and failure. It has been a joy to feature Alex Depledge, Anjali Ramachandran, Anne-Marie Imafidon, Anurag Acharya, Cara Holland, Carolina Martins, Charlotte Cramer, Dave Gray, George Bettany, George Burgess, Gunita Bhasin, Howard Kingston, Jane Haslett Evans, Jenn Maer, Jennifer Aldrich, Jeremy Greaves, Jessica Livingston, Jo Caley, John Kershaw, Jon Bradford, Mariana Marquez, Mohammad Al-Ubadyli, Nicole Raby, Paul-Jervis Heath, Rob Fitzpatrick, Sally Lait, Sam Reid, Sarah Drinkwater, Vix Anderton and Wil Benton. I am thankful and humbled by Vikas Shah for his foreword to the book. It's been an honour to share the work of Angela Duckworth, Ash Maurya, Clayton Christensen, David Kelley, Eric Ries, Jake Knapp, Martin Seligman, Pascal Finette, Tom Kelley and the many other researchers and experts who have inspired my work in innovation over the years.

I tested lots of elements of the book with beta readers whose feedback on the contents, cover design and early drafts kept me focussed on audience needs. I am grateful to Anna Giulia Novero, Anna Slodka, Caroline Curtis, Cecilia Thirlway, Gunita Bhasin, Ilona Leighton Goodall, James Friel, Jo Wood, John Lugo-Trebble, Kat Palmer, Liz Flanagan, Mark Watkins, Rebecca Stockdale, Sally Lait and Sue Burkett for reading the first draft. Your comments, feedback and constructive criticism transformed the book. I am grateful to others in the beta group for their feedback, support and encouragement, including Andy Canty, Andy Ireland, Bailey Kursar, Bekka Prideaux, Catherine Williams, Clare Painter, Danielle Ormshaw, Dee Watchorn, Gareth Bell, George Palmer, Sharon Jones, Stephanie Michaux, Steve King, Sue Bramhall, Suki Fuller and Tom Clark.

A very warm thank you to my bosses, colleagues, clients and the hundreds of participants who have taken part in my workshops over the years, to those who read my blogs and articles, also to the students, founders and ideas makers I have mentored and coached. Thank you for your patience as I developed my approach and for allowing me to experiment and fail better.

Shout out to the Salisbury Roaders, especially Catherine Smith and Sarah Manfredi for celebrating every book milestone. Sarah Birnie for gifting me her house to write in last summer. I am also thankful to Gladstone's Library and Hebden Bridge Town Hall for providing distraction-free writing boltholes when I most needed them. My siblings Matthew, Imogen, Dominic and Tristan for keeping it real – thank you for stopping me taking myself too seriously, for building my resilience with relentless teasing, and for making me laugh and feel loved. My Mum for reading every single draft of the book; providing tea, cake, a quiet place to write, the encouragement to keep going and the criticism to be better; and for providing synonyms for every single swear word I used. Thank you, Dad, for always believing I could do it.

I owe all the good things in my life to Chris – he brings the happy to all my hustles. Without him this book would not exist.

PERMISSIONS

Every effort has been made to contact the copyright holders of the material reproduced in this book. If any have been inadvertently overlooked, the publisher will be pleased to make acknowledgement on future editions if notified.

Empathy Map Canvas © 2017 Dave Gray, xplane.com

'The Tough Room – Act 1 The Onion', *This American Life* © This American Life, quotes used with permission.

'Moonshots' and 'Fall in love with the problem" from *The Heretic* are licensed under the Creative Commons Attribution CC-BY-NC license and used with permission of the author Pascal Finette.

UI / UX bicycle Doodle © userexperiencerocks.com reprinted with permission from Jennifer Aldrich.

Design Sprint weekly overview © Jake Knapp, reprinted by permission of the author.

Lean Canvas is adapted from the Business Model Canvas and is licensed under the Creative Commons Attribution-Share Alike 3.0 Un-ported License. © LeanStack, reprinted with permission from Ash Maurya.

Growth curve © Escape Velocity, reprinted with permission from Howard Kingston.

Revised Technology Adoption Cycle, used by permission from Geoffrey A. Moore's *Crossing the Chasm, 3rd Edition* © 1991, 1999, 2002, 2014 by Geoffrey A. Moore.

Original illustrations in this book are by Cara Holland and may not be reproduced without permission from the publisher.

Notes

Introduction

1   Mill, John Stuart. *Autobiography*, Project Gutenberg, 2003. http://www.gutenberg.org/files/10378/10378-h/10378-h.htm

2   Wieth, Mareike B. and Zacks, Rose T. 'Time of day effects on problem solving: When the non-optimal is optimal.' *Thinking & Reasoning*, Vol. 17, No. 4 (2011), 387–401, https://doi.org/10.1080/13546783.2011.625663.

Chapter 1

3   Mintel. 'Online fashion clicks with brits as market increases 152% over past five years.' 15 April 2011. http://www.mintel.com/press-centre/fashion/online-fashion-clicks-with-brits-as-market-increases-152-over-past-five-years.

4   Graham, Paul. 'How to get startup ideas.' November 2012. http://paulgraham.com/startupideas.html.

5   Kelley, David and Kelley, Tom. *Creative Confidence: Unleashing the Creative Potential Within Us All.* Crown Business, 2015, 22.

6   Credit for this exercise goes to Claire Merrick, ex-head of innovation for multinational oil and gas company BP. She took her own advice to discover new interests – after dabbling with acting on the side, she quit her corporate routine to pursue a career as an actor and voiceover artist.

7   Duckworth, Angela. *Grit: The Power of Passion and Perseverance.* Vermilion, 2016, 104.

8   Panksepp, Jaak. *Affective Neuroscience: The Foundations of Human and Animal Emotions.* Oxford University Press, 2004, 52.

9   Levy, Steven. 'The Gentleman Who Made Scholar.' *Wired*, 17 October 2014. https://www.wired.com/2014/10/the-gentleman-who-made-scholar.

Chapter 2

10   Burnett, Bill and Evans, Dave. *Designing Your Life: Build a Life that Works for You*. Vintage, 2018, xix.

11   Kelley, David and Kelley, Tom. *Creative Confidence: Unleashing the Creative Potential Within Us All*. Crown Business, 2015, 21.

12   The XPLANE Collection. 'The Updated Empathy Map Canvas.' 15 July 2017. https://medium.com/the-xplane-collection/updated-empathy-map-canvas-46df22df3c8a.

13   Gamestorming. 'Empathy Map.' 12 November 2009. http://gamestorming.com/empathy-map.

Chapter 3

14   The Heretic. 'Moonshots (or: How to Solve the World's Biggest Problems).' 19 October 2016. https://read.theheretic.org/moonshots-or-how-to-solve-the-worlds-biggest-problems-e142c89b5837

15   Google. 'Our mission is to organize the world's information and make it universally accessible and useful.' https://www.google.com/about.

16   The Heretic. 'Fall in Love With The Problem.' 3 July 2016. https://read.theheretic.org/fall-in-love-with-the-problem-f9fe915eb291.

17   Nutt, Paul C. *Why Decisions Fail: Avoiding the Blunders and Traps That Lead to Debacles*. Berrett-Koehler Publishers Inc, 2002, 7.

18   Nutt, Paul C. *Why Decisions Fail: Avoiding the Blunders and Traps That Lead to Debacles*. Berrett-Koehler Publishers Inc, 2002, 363.

19   Carroll, Rory. 'David Lynch: "You gotta be selfish. It's a terrible thing".' *Guardian*, 23 June 2018. https://www.theguardian.com/film/2018/jun/23/david-lynch-gotta-be-selfish-twin-peaks.

20   Beaty, Roger; Kenett, Yoed; Christensen, Alexander;
     Rosenberg, Monica; Benedek, Mathias; Chen, Qunlin;
     Fink, Andreas; Qiu, Jiang; Kwapil, Thomas; Kane,
     Michael; and Silvia, Paul. 'Robust Prediction of
     Individual Creative Ability from Brain Functional
     Connectivity.' *Proceedings of the National Academy
     of Sciences*, Vol. 115, No. 5 (2018) 1087–92, https://doi.
     org/10.1073/pnas.1713532115.

21   IDEO. 'Designing a School System from the Ground
     Up.' 2014. https://www.ideo.com/case-study/designing-
     a-school-system-from-the-ground-up.

22   Berger, Warren. 'The Secret Phrase Top Innovators
     Use.' *Harvard Business Review*, 17 September 2012.
     https://hbr.org/2012/09/the-secret-phrase-top-innovato.

23   To find out more about 'How might we …' statements,
     check out IDEO's design kit and the full exercise,
     http://www.designkit.org/methods/3.

24   'Throughout the experiments, the items participants
     listed under "unconscious thought" conditions
     were more original. It was concluded that whereas
     conscious thought may be focussed and convergent,
     unconscious thought may be more associative and
     divergent.' Dijksterhuis, Ap and Meurs, Teun.
     'Where creativity resides: The generative power of
     unconscious thought.' *Consciousness and Cognition*,
     Vol. 15, No. 1 (2006), 135–46, https://doi.org/10.1016/j.
     concog.2005.04.007.

25   Brain and creativity expert Tony Buzan popularised
     mind maps in the 1960s. He says that through daily
     use of this tool 'you will find that your life becomes
     more productive, fulfilled, and successful on every
     level'. Find out more https://www.tonybuzan.com.

26   For creative warm-ups, check out the Gamestorming
     website or book: Gray, Dave; Brown, Sunni; and
     Macanufo, James. *Gamestorming: A Playbook for
     Innovators, Rulebreakers, and Changemakers*.
     O'Reilly Media, 2010.

Chapter 4

27 'The Tough Room.' *This American Life*, February 2008, https://www.thisamericanlife.org/348/tough-room.

28 'In writing, you must kill all your darlings.' Said by William Faulkner and quoted by Stephen King who advised writers: 'Kill your darlings, kill your darlings, even when it breaks your egocentric little scribbler's heart, kill your darlings.'

29 Nemeth, Charlan J.; Personnaz, Bernard; Personnaz, Marie; and Goncalo, Jack A.; 'The liberating role of conflict in group creativity: A study in two countries.' *European Journal of Social Psychology*, Vol. 34, No. 4 (2004), 365–74, https://doi.org/10.1002/ejsp.210.

30 Nutt, Paul C. *Why Decisions Fail: Avoiding the Blunders and Traps That Lead to Debacles.* Berrett-Koehler Publishers Inc, 2002.

31 Iyengar, Sheena, S. and Lepper, Mark. 'When Choice is Demotivating: Can One Desire Too Much of a Good Thing?' *Journal of Personality and Social Psychology*, Vol. 79, No. 6 (2000), 995–1006, http://dx.doi.org/10.1037/0022-3514.79.6.995

32 This is known as the HiPPO in the room – when the Highest Paid Person's Opinion over rules everyone else.

33 If you're worried about populism and fancy a spot of electoral reform to allow independent ideas to thrive, go for a single transferable vote, which will give you a winner based on the strength of support for the idea.

34 Gollwitzer, Peter M. and Oettingen, Gabriele. 'The emergence and implementation of health goals.' *Psychology and Health*, Vol. 13, No. 4 (1998), 687–715, https://doi.org/10.1080/08870449808407424.

35 Author's calculation based on 600 headlines a week over 30 years is close to a million.

Chapter 5

36   Design Sprints. 'Crazy 8's.' https://designsprintkit.
     withgoogle.com/methods/sketch/crazy-8s.
37   Holland, Cara. *Draw a Better Business*. Practical
     Inspiration Publishing, 2018.
38   User Experience Rocks, the blog of Jennifer Aldrich.
     https://userexperiencerocks.wordpress.com/

Chapter 6

39   *The Tim Ferriss Show*. 'The Man Who Taught Me
     How to Invest – Mike Maples.' (#286), 2018, https://tim.
     blog/2018/02/04/the-tim-ferriss-show-transcripts-mike-
     maples.
40   Strack, F., Martin, L.L. and Stepper, S. 'Inhibiting
     and facilitating conditions of the human smile:
     A nonobtrusive test of the facial feedback
     hypothesis.' *Journal of Personality and Social
     Psychology,* Vol. 54, No. 5 (1988), 768–77. https://doi.
     org/10.1177/1745691616674458.
41   Cuddy, Amy. 'Your Body Language May Shape Who
     You Are.' Filmed at TEDGlobal June 2012. https://
     www.ted.com/talks/amy_cuddy_your_body_language_
     shapes_who_you_are.

Chapter 7

42   Lawless, John. 'Revealed: the eight-year-old girl who
     saved Harry Potter.' *The Independent,* 3 July 2005.
     https://www.independent.co.uk/arts-entertainment/
     books/news/revealed-the-eight-year-old-girl-who-
     saved-harry-potter-296456.html.
43   Startup Lessons Learned by Eric Ries. 'Minimum
     Viable Product: a guide.' 3 August 2009.
     http://www.startuplessonslearned.com/2009/08/
     minimum-viable-product-guide.html.
44   Schauer, Brandon. 'Cupcakes: the secret to product
     planning.' *Adaptive Path,* 10 February 2011.
     http://adaptivepath.org/ideas/cupcakes-the-secret-to-
     product-planning

45   Partnoy, Frank. *Wait: The useful art of procrastination*. Profile Books, 2012.

46   *The Startup Podcast*. 'Fake It Til You Make It.' *Gimlet Media*, 2 February 2015. https://www.gimletmedia. com/startup/13-fake-it-til-you-make-it#episode-player

47   Knapp, Jake with Zeratsky, John and Kowitz, Braden. *Sprint: Solve Big Problems and Test New Ideas in Just Five Days*. Bantam Press, 2016.

48   Evans, Bec. 'What traditional publishers can learn from design sprints.' *GV Sprint Stories*, 7 June 2016. https://sprintstories.com/what-traditional-publishers-can-learn-from-design-sprints-76f7c9c91e8.

Chapter 8

49   Innocent Drinks. 'Hello we're Innocent.' https://www.innocentdrinks.co.uk/us/our-story.

50   Apologies to all scientists. I am going to use data as both a single and a plural. This will cause you pain, but I'd rather pain than datum.

51   Fitzpatrick, Rob. *The Mom Test: How to talk to customers and learn if your business is a good idea when everyone is lying to you*. Founder Centric, 2014, 11.

52   Smith, Chris. 'If nobody pays for apps anymore, how did we get 16 per cent of our users to pay a tenner for a prototype?' 10 January 2018. https://blog.prototypr. io/if-nobody-pays-for-apps-anymore-how-did-we-get-16-of-our-users-to-pay-a-tenner-for-a-prototype-f41051b32472.

53   Find out more about the Net Promoter Score https://www.netpromoter.com/know.

54   Uber. 'About.' Accessed August 2018. https://www.uber. com/en-GB.

55   Gray, Dave. *Selling to the VP of NO*. XPLANE Corp. Kindle Edition, 2015.

56   Alex Osterwalder created the Business Model Canvas which is licensed under Creative Commons through his company Strategyzer https://strategyzer.com/ canvas/business-model-canvas.

57   Maurya, Ash. 'Why Lean Canvas vs Business Model
     Canvas?' *Love the Problem* blog by the makers
     of LEANSTACK, 27 February 2012. https://blog.
     leanstack.com/why-lean-canvas-vs-business-model-
     canvas-af62c0f250f0.

58   The Lean Canvas, Licensed under Creative Commons,
     reproduced with permission of Ash Maurya of
     LEANSTACK. https://leanstack.com/is-one-page-
     business-model.

59   Christensen, Clayton. 'The "Jobs to be Done" Theory
     of Innovation.' *Harvard Business Review* Ideacast, 8
     December 2016. https://hbr.org/ideacast/2016/12/the-
     jobs-to-be-done-theory-of-innovation.

Chapter 9

60   Grossman, David. 'Secret Google lab "rewards staff
     for failure".' BBC Newsnight, 24 January 2014.
     http://www.bbc.co.uk/news/technology-25880738

61   X Company – The Moonshot Factory. Accessed 5
     September 2017. https://x.company/about.

62   Blank, Steve. 'Why the Lean Start-Up Changes
     Everything.' *Harvard Business Review*, May 2013.
     https://hbr.org/2013/05/why-the-lean-start-up-changes-
     everything.

63   Robertson-Kraft, Claire and Duckworth, Angela L.
     'True Grit: Perseverance and Passion for Long-term
     Goals Predicts Effectiveness and Retention Among
     Novice Teachers.' *Teachers College Record*, 116
     (2014), 1–24.

64   'More than 90 per cent of startups fail, due primarily
     to self-destruction rather than competition.' *Startup
     Genome Report Extra on Premature Scaling: A
     deep dive into why most high growth startups fail*,
     29 August 2011. http://innovationfootprints.com/wp-
     content/uploads/2015/07/startup-genome-report-extra-
     on-premature-scaling.pdf.

65   Fitzpatrick, Rob. *The Mom Test: How to talk to
     customers and learn if your business is a good idea
     when everyone is lying to you.* Founder Centric,
     2014, 39–41.

66   Epictetus. *Discourses* 3.10.2–3.

67   Lyubomirsky, S., Sousa, L. and Dickerhoof, R. 'The costs and benefits of writing, talking, and thinking about life's triumphs and defeats.' *Journal of Personality and Social Psychology,* Vol. 90, No. 4 (2006), 692–708 http://dx.doi.org/10.1037/0022-3514.90.4.692.

68   Seligman, M. E.; Steen, T.A.; Park, N.; and Peterson, C. 'Empirical Validation of Interventions.' *American Psychologist.* Vol. 60, No. 1 (2005), 410–21 https://doi.org/10.1037/0003-066X.60.5.410.

69   Grant, A. M. and Gino, F. 'A Little Thanks Goes a Long Way: Explaining Why Gratitude Expressions Motivate Prosocial Behavior.' *Journal of Personality and Social Psychology.* Vol. 98, No. 6 (2010), 946–55 http://dx.doi.org/10.1037/a0017935.

70   'What I Learned from Spanx Founder Sara Blakely.' James Altucher Show, episode 211. http://www.jamesaltucher.com/2017/02/sara-blakely.

71   Dweck, Carol. *Mindset: The New Psychology of Success.* Ballantine Books, 2007.

Chapter 10

72   Golson, Jordan. 'Well, that didn't work: The Segway is a technological marvel. Too bad it doesn't make any sense.' *Wired,* 16 January 2015. https://www.wired.com/2015/01/well-didnt-work-segway-technological-marvel-bad-doesnt-make-sense.

73   Hamer, M.; Stamatakis, E.; and Steptoe, A. 'Dose-response relationship between physical activity and mental health: the Scottish Health Survey.' *British Journal of Sports Medicine,* Vol. 43 (2009), 1111–14. https://bjsm.bmj.com/content/43/14/1111.

74   Sloan, D.M.; Sawyer, A.T.; Lowmaster, S.E. et al. 'Efficacy of Narrative Writing as an Intervention for PTSD: Does the Evidence Support Its Use?' *Journal of Contemporary Psychotherapy,* Vol. 45, No. 4 (2015), 215–25. https://link.springer.com/article/10.1007%2Fs10879-014-9292-x.

75   Branson, Richard. 'How to Succeed at Failure.' *Daily Monitor*, 5 October 2010. 'Over the years, my team and I have not let mistakes, failures or mishaps get us down. Instead, even when a venture has failed, we try to look for opportunities, to see whether we can capitalise on another gap in the market.' https://www.monitor.co.ug/Business/Prosper/688616-1025658-gw6k2y/index.html

76   Beckett, Samuel. *Worstward Ho*. Grove Press, 1983, 7.

77   Duckworth, Angela. *Grit: The Power of Passion and Perseverance*. Vermilion, 2016, 86.

Chapter 11

78   Paul Graham quotes *The Journals of Ralph Waldo Emerson, 1849–1855* in his blog *Do Things That Don't Scale*, http://paulgraham.com/ds.html.

79   Ellis, Sean. 'The Startup Pyramid.' http://www.startup-marketing.com/the-startup-pyramid.

80   Moore, Geoffrey A. *Crossing the Chasm. Harper Business*. Third Edition, 2014, 7–8.

81   Godin, Seth. 'The Tribes We Lead.' TED2009. Filmed at an official TED conference in February 2009. https://www.ted.com/talks/seth_godin_on_the_tribes_we_lead.

82   'Go Back to What Lights Your Heart on Fire: This is What Makes a Hit.' James Altucher Show, episode 376 with Seth Godin. https://jamesaltucher.com/category/the-james-altucher-show.

83   Kelly, Kevin. '1000 True Fans.' 2008. Kelly defined a fan as somebody that will buy anything you produce. 'To make a living as a craftsperson, photographer, musician, designer, author, animator, app maker, entrepreneur, or inventor you need only thousands of true fans.' https://kk.org/thetechnium/1000-true-fans.

84   McBratney, Sam and Jeram, Anita. *Guess How Much I Love You*. Walker Books, 2007.

85   McClure, Dave. 'Startup Metrics for Pirates: AARRR!!!' This is a five-step model for creating a metrics framework for your business and customers, and how

to apply it to your product and marketing efforts. The 'pirate' part comes from the five steps: Acquisition, Activation, Retention, Referral, and Revenue (AARRR!). https://www.slideshare.net/dmc500hats/startup-metrics-for-pirates-long-version

Chapter 12

86   Bellah, Robert N.; Madsen, Richard; Sullivan, William M.; Swidler, Ann; and Tipton, Steven M. *Habits of the Heart: Individualism and Commitment in American Life*. University of California Press, 1985.

87   Wrzesniewski, Amy; McCauley, Clark; Rozin, Paul; and Schwartz, Barry. 'Jobs, Careers, and Callings: People's Relations to Their Work.' *Journal of Research in Personality*. Vol. 31, No. 1 (March 1997), 21–33
https://doi.org/10.1006/jrpe.1997.2162.

88   Guillebeau, Chris. *Side Hustle: Build a Side Business and Make Extra Money – Without Quitting Your Day Job*. Macmillan, 2017.

89   Side Hustle School. 'About.' https://sidehustleschool.com/about.

90   Cohen, Susan G. 'Accelerating Startups: The Seed Accelerator Phenomenon.' March 2014, http://seedrankings.com/pdf/seed-accelerator-phenomenon.pdf.

91   Hathaway, Ian. 'What Startup Accelerators Really Do.' *Harvard Business Review*, 1 March 2016, https://hbr.org/2016/03/what-startup-accelerators-really-do.

92   Y Combinator. Accessed August 2018. http://www.ycombinator.com.

93   Livingston, Jessica. 'Grow the Puzzle Around You.' 30 June 2018. http://foundersatwork.posthaven.com/grow-the-puzzle-around-you

Conclusion

94   Murray, C. B. and Peacock, M. J. 'A model-free approach to the study of subjective wellbeing.' In H. W. Neighbors and J. S. Jackson (Eds.), *Mental Health*

in Black America, Thousand Oaks: Sage Publications, 1996, 14–26.

95 Volpicelli, Gian. 'What do you do when you've made £27m cleaning? Get into home extensions.' *Wired*, August 4, 2017. https://www.wired.co.uk/article/hassle-founders-alex-depledge-jules-coleman-buildpath-home-extensions.

96 Christakis, Nicholas A. and James H. Fowler. 'The spread of obesity in a large social network over 32 years.' *The New England Journal of Medicine*. Vol. 357, No. 4. (2007) 370–9. https://www.nejm.org/doi/full/10.1056/NEJMsa066082.

97 Records Sound the Same. 'Case study: part-time CTO support and mentoring with Prolifiko.' October 27, 2017. https://recordssoundthesame.com/blog/2017/10/27/prolifiko-cto-support-and-mentoring.

98 Shah, Vikas. 'How to Save your Own Life.' Filmed at TEDxManchester, February 11, 2018 https://www.youtube.com/watch?v=hrSq-85D8dg

99 Positive Psychology Program. 'The PERMA Model: Your Scientific Theory of Happiness.' February 24, 2017. https://positivepsychologyprogram.com/perma-model.

100 Duckworth, Angela. *Grit: The Power of Passion and Perseverance*. Vermilion, 2016, 50.

101 Watts, Alan. 'The Hoax.' 1966. Animated version by Furry Carlos Productions, made by Trey Parker and Matt Stone, the creators of *South Park*, https://www.youtube.com/watch?v=WGoTmNU_5A0.

BEFORE YOU GO

Thanks for reading *How to Have a Happy Hustle*. Before you go, here are three things you can do.

1. If you enjoyed the book, please take the time to **review it on Goodreads or Amazon**. Doing this helps other people find the book and will mean a lot to me too. Thank you! :)

2. Now you're determined to make your idea happen, **sign up to my newsletter at happyhustlebook.com** where you can book on to my courses, workshops and events. You can also hire me as a coach, facilitator or speaker.

3. If you'd like my help supercharging your writing project, go to **prolifiko.com** where you can find out about our amazing coaching plans.

Bec Evans
Twitter/Instagram @Eva_Bec